SOUL FORCE

RELEASING THE POWER TO MAKE THE REST OF YOUR LIFE WORK

By Dr. Paul Olsen

M Evans
Lanham • New York • Boulder • Toronto • Plymouth, UK

M Evans
An imprint of Rowman & Littlefield
4501 Forbes Boulevard, Suite 200
Lanham, Maryland 20706
www.rowman.com

10 Thornbury Road, Plymouth PL6 7PP
United Kingdom

Library of Congress Cataloging in Publication Data

Olsen, Paul.
  Soul force.

  Bibliography: p.
  1. Success. I. Title.
  BF637.S8046   158'.1   78-18500
  ISBN 978-1-59077-308-6

Distributed by
NATIONAL BOOK NETWORK

Design by Ginger Giles

Manufactured in the United States of America

9 8 7 6 5 4 3 2 1

For Deborah

With whom the word was shaped . . .

I want to say thanks with much love to Martha Winston, who has been my literary agent since 1957. After twenty years of complete unwavering faith in me, her retirement has ended a professional relationship of great meaning to me. But it can't end what I feel personally about her. To me, a beautiful and wonderful lady.

Thanks also to Herbert M. Katz, who seems always to *be there,* as editor and friend, when I need to write.

And to my clients I owe an incalculable debt for their involvement in my humanity. I merely want to add that their anonymity has been scrupulously preserved. As I said once, in another place, I doubt if they would recognize the "facts" of their lives. But it is the meaning that matters, the spirit that counts, and not the facts.

Contents

Foreword

There is a time, I know, when a human being can fall so deeply into the dark night of the soul that his eyes must open to a light or stay shut for eternity.

I will never forget Lama Anagarika Govinda leaning forward from his perch of pillows like some gentle, exquisite, life-drenched bird, an inner flame igniting his eyes —leaning forward, raising his steepled fingers, and saying:

If only we can hold the light. . . .

There is Deborah who held her lantern aloft searching for what is honest and true.

Marissa and Matthew, whose souls are always ablaze.

Estelle and Elliot Rinzler who helped so much in the kindling of it all.

And even Kitty and Cootie Bug, whose tiny rays play into the small dark corners.

If only we can hold the light.

1
Rediscovering the Soul

"The lightning shot down, bolt after bolt, like spears thrown from the sky, and just as they were about to strike the water they seemed to burst and spread out in flat sheets of light. They lit up the darkness, night turned to day for whole seconds at a time. I could see clear across the bay to the island, and once a pocket of flame and smoke exploded in the trees, sucking the lightning bolt into it. The wind, the driving rain—they whipped against my face until I had to squint. But I kept forcing my eyes open because I needed to keep seeing. And suddenly the whole sky burst into a great white light and I could somehow see straight into the end of time. I could see the beginning and the end of everything in the brief shattering of that darkness, in that explosion of light.

"For a moment I had no idea if what I had just experienced was something that had really occurred in the sky, or if it had burst forth inside me. Maybe it was both—both at the same time.

"And then I began to laugh, and my tears mixed with the rain streaming down my face.

"Because I had the unshakable knowledge that I would never again be afraid."

THE SEARCH FOR A SOUL

This is Mark: his words. He told me of this experience at the end of a summer, a month before he ended psycho-therapy with me.

But to understand how he got to his final "unshakable knowledge," we have to go back a bit in time, to the end of another summer—when something was missing. . . .

It is his first session of that September. Mark is in his early thirties, tanned, dressed to show his success, and he feels a need to catalogue things as if he has been away for much longer than a month. A kind of personal inventory. His words go something like this:

"I don't think I really have any problems with women and I think I'm going to get my raise. . . . I guess you could say my summer was good."

He thinks, guesses; he doesn't seem to *know*.

"I'll probably be making enough next year to buy into a half share of the summer house. . . ."

He fades off and stares out the window. His face looks suddenly pained, then puzzled; the space gives me time to think about his catalogue. In terms of our social goals it all seems exciting. But his tone is flat, even a bit dead.

Now he tells me that he is depressed—"or something." And finally: "It's like—I don't know. Like I don't have a soul." Quickly· "That was stupid. I don't know why I said that."

Years ago I wouldn't have understood him—not really. I would have agreed that he was just depressed—"or something." But these days I know what he means, and his use of the word *soul* is strong to me. It resonates deep inside.

"Why is it stupid?" I ask.

"It sounds like something in Sunday School."

"Is that how it feels to you?"

"No. It feels empty, like something big is missing—like I have no soul. I can't say it any better."

He doesn't have to say it any better. It's exactly what it is, what it feels like.

So here he is: bright, young, successful with work and women, a picture of achievement to the outside world. But something is horribly wrong. He feels he has no soul, and so feels that he is not a whole person, empty, not fully alive.

Suddenly he begins to cry, and I have a feeling that he is going to tell himself something that, in my own way, in my own time and place, I have told myself. And then it happens: in *his* way, *his* language.

"What the hell does it do me? I have all these *things*. The beach house is a thing, my car is a thing, even women are things. I feel like a bunch of disconnected parts—like a mess of arms and legs and guts and thoughts, and I can't find the glue. I'm in pieces. Christ! I see *myself* as a thing. Some kind of thing all broken up into pieces."

He doesn't know it yet, but he is about to embark on a journey that will make science fiction seem like *The Three Little Bears*.

He cries again and I don't interrupt. For me it is always a touching, powerful, and beautiful experience when a man in our society can confront himself and let himself cry. It is always life-giving. In sessions it is a strong clue that therapy is truly moving, that change is occurring. The tears from the center push through the mask. The tears will probably be the raw stuff of the glue he looks for.

Without effort my thoughts turn by themselves to another client of mine who shortly before our first meeting suffered a heart attack that immobilized him for months. He was also "successful"—but it all came pouring out of him in the same kind of torrent, again in *his* way, *his* style. What was different about him was his deep automatic decision to leave the world as he had known it before he could begin to create his own real world, a world that had meaning for him. Part of it was:

"I can't go to those parties any more. Everybody wants to know what you *do.* If it's not what they want to hear, if it's not jazzy or 'with it' or 'important'—whatever the hell *that* means—it's like their eyes go out. Like you threw a switch and the bulbs burned out. They need to get away from you so they don't waste their time. You feel dead, like you don't matter. That's the hell of it—that you feel *you* don't matter when somebody else splits on you."

The important thing about this man is that he doesn't give up, or turn bitter, or become a cynic or a pessimist. He lets go of an old way of existing for a new life of inner experience and inner strength. He needed to face death for a time, but that's what it took to bring *him* to *his* soul. Unlike Mark, he has never used the word, but he doesn't have to; the word itself, like all words, is just a shorthand. It's the sense of it that counts—a sense of the most powerful and dynamic energy a human being can experience when he liberates it from its prison within.

Significantly, both these men are successful as we define the term in the everyday world. There is nothing wrong with that kind of success—if it stays in perspective, where it belongs, and doesn't become either everything or a substitute for something else. Others, when they discover the soul within, can become successful in that way simply because they don't *have* to cut such a possibility from their lives.

Many people, when they hear the word *soul,* immediately set it up as some sort of opposition to material things —even to the whole world of materiality. As if one cannot have both. As if materialism is "bad" or destructive simply because it is there.

No one wears hairshirts these days. And it takes a knowledge and grasp of the materialistic world before we can live in it with any sort of ease and meaning.

To search for the soul, to rediscover it, has nothing to do with the need to give up, or to put down, materialism or worldly success. We simply are finally able to put it into perspective, to lend it balance. We want to *use* material things, to enjoy them; and with balance we can. With balance, we control materiality. It no longer controls us by being the only goal we can see in our lives. Success ceases to be a place to which *we must get at all costs.* It becomes a part of life—not the major focus of life.

With balance we no longer let our drive for success dominate us. Nor do we suffer the agonies of hell when we are temporarily blocked from it. We become aware of the process, of our energy. Our success *becomes us,* not some goal *out there.*

Success can be very natural, almost a reflex. . . .

Mark tries to compose himself, but he is fighting his tears now. So I ask him if he is really finished crying—or is it that he thinks he *should* stop. He cries some more and lets it end when it is ready to.

Soul.

While I felt it strongly that day, it wasn't until I got home that I could think of it, focus on the soul and what it has meant for me to recognize, discover, and touch it within myself. And when I focus on it, I see my history, my life as it once was.

OPENING POSSIBILITIES

My recognition of my soul has changed every aspect of my life—or maybe better said, the recognition has removed, and continues to remove, the blocks and illusions that once dammed up the natural flow of my life. My relationships to people are totally different, and so is my work—work being different because I no longer see it as work. So what I really mean is that the way I see myself and the world has radically changed through a process of personal evolution, and the world continually holds new possibilities for me.

New possibilities might even seem terribly trivial—but not when you compare them with your past, locked-in, robot-like behavior and reactions. Then they are very important: because you see and feel the change within yourself. No thought, no plan, no effort. Simply a flow. Here's partly what I mean:

For years I've had an infrequent correspondence with a very angry person. His letters have usually been abusive and hostile, and in the past they always got to me. My own anger would begin to ignite the moment I saw the familiar handwriting on the envelope in the mailbox—and already teed off, the contents were like a bomb that could only make the whole situation blow up. It would literally ruin my day.

Not so long ago there was the envelope nestled in the

box. Taking it out (not extracting it by a corner with my thumb and forefinger as I used to do), I was suddenly not angry at all—or better put, the letter didn't infect my balanced mood. I read it then and there. It reeked with the usual abuse, but for the first time it had no effect on me. More, for the first time I became aware that the anger was masking a number of very human requests, and that this person did not have any other human being to whom he felt he could even *show* his anger.

I answered the letter without once alluding to his angry tone, without once getting involved in the abusive game. And I think I gave him a little bit of what he wanted or needed in the process.

None of this was the least bit planned. It just happened.

Later, when I showed a friend my reply, she asked: "How long did it take you to write this?"

"Over forty years," I answered.

Everything changes when you recognize your soul. Because *it is that big*. It is all of you.

For the first time in my life I feel that I can see more of the reality of things, for the first time I am not living in a world of make-believe and mistaking it for what truly *is*.

When I was stuck in that world and hating much of it, yet looking *very* successful in the eyes of others, I might have gagged on the word *soul*. I know I would have gotten angry—a strong residue of my Catholic upbringing and being pushed around by teachers and rules. In *my* eyes they all seemed more interested in "good behavior" than in the soul, more interested in keeping you afraid than in helping you discover your meaning. Again, that's how *I* saw it.

I left that structure as time passed, but for a long while I would cling to the false belief that the soul was a purely religious idea, even a religious *thing*—along the lines of those miniature paintings of medieval times in which some saint holds in the palms of his hands a soul that resembles a tiny white person. In other words, I missed the point: that soul is not the property of any organized religion, neither Christian, Jewish, Islamic, whatever.

And it is certainly not something that appears only after our bodies die.

Because everybody "has" one, everybody *is* one, no matter what faith you believe or don't believe in. You don't have to belong to anything, or do anything, to have one. It just *is*. And what it is, is everything that connects us to ourselves, to others, to everything that exists. It is what connects us right now: not the words on this page, or the content, or the idea that I write in English and you understand it. What is really connecting us right now is the ability of our souls to interplay. First that, *then* the words. We are having contact right now.

Soul is the energy that propels life, the energy in all living things. Soul is why you can love not only your lover, your spouse, your child, but also why you can love an animal or a plant, or feel love for a character in a novel or a play, even though that character is supposed to be "fictional." It is why you can cry in response to music that has no words, no lyrics; why you can be beautifully hypnotized by staring into a fire. It is how you love and respect yourself and it is via the soul that you give yourself the possibilities through which you can begin to glimpse the meaning of all life.

The problem is, as we grow up the soul becomes banked like a coal fire whose embers barely glow. And then when we feel the need for meaning in our later years, we are first surprised by this need—and then almost always look in the wrong place to quench the need. It may take a lot of work—at first—to rediscover the soul.

SOUL SEARCH

The term "soul-searching" means exactly what it says—one of those essential expressions that gets twisted from real meaning into a cliché. Yet look at it for a moment, don't pass it by or dismiss it. (Not seeing what is right under our noses keeps us away from ourselves; and part of the journey to discovering the soul is looking at old things as if they never existed before.) See its meaning, see why it exists at all: that when you want to find something of value, of importance, the place to go is inside yourself, not out. Into the core of yourself where there are no masks—not outside somewhere where almost everything is masked.

To acquaint yourself with the sense that to some degree almost everything wears a mask, look at the vocabulary we use and accept without question. We *accept* that people have "roles": a role at home, a role at work, myriad roles so refined that we play a subtly different one with every person we know. And we get to play roles with ourselves.

Why do we accept this in others and in ourselves?

From this point on, let's try not to accept anything that smacks of the following old defense: "That's life—that's the way people are."

Okay. I personally have never had a true relationship while I maintained a role. And I *know* that I never did a decent piece of therapeutic work until I peeled off the façade and self-image of "doctor." And until I stopped seeing people as "patients."

The great danger of masks is that we come to believe

that they are not just protective devices; we get to believe that our masks *are* us.

We are going to try to peel away a lot of masks via the "Explorations" in this book, by observing something about masks and truth in a very direct way.

Let's ease into it.

EXPLORATION: Briefly focus on the roles you play with a number of important people in your life. Your wife or husband, your lover, your boss, your neighbor, your parents. Different, aren't they? There's a lack of consistency. This is not social adaptation. This is a wrenching of your character into an emotional pretzel. It's what causes the strain, the tiredness, the anxiety that you can never quite put your finger on.

Socially now, you can try the following experiment and discover what develops.

EXPLORATION: Just say to someone you know, a friend or acquaintance:

"I want to tell you a truth about yourself."

Watch what happens.

The odds are at least a conservative 1,000,000 to one that the other person will immediately become defensive and nervous, even angry. You will see it in the eyes, the change in posture, the words—all of it.

Because when someone tells us that he is going to reveal a truth about ourselves, we instantaneously think it will be negative. Just the possibility of truth will be taken as an attack. The suspicious emphasis on "the truth hurts" can make liars of us all.

Be sure that, after you observe the reaction, you tell this person a *positive* truth about him or her—for example, "You make it very easy for people to get close to you"—or whatever else might be true.

We have so much of everything backwards. The possibility of the truth—*even only the possibility*—scares us most of the time. Our defensive reactions—like the ones I predicted in the last Exploration—indicate that we think we don't know something about ourselves. Yet only *we* can *really* know, even if at first we think we don't: real knowledge, like the soul itself, is often hard to see.

But you *can* get to see it. There are no tricks, no gimmicks. All you have to do is *see*. We will get very deeply into *seeing*.

At this point I realize that I've already touched a lot of bases, but I'd like to set the tone. I'll elaborate, so that there is as little mystery as possible about the soul. (Just remember that it is a total self-connection.) And you will meet a lot of people in this book, myself included—friends, associates, but especially the people who come to me for help, often because they feel anxious or depressed or just "missing something," only to find out that what they needed was not advice or a pat on the head or some long bouts of intellectual discussion. What they needed—what we all need—is themselves, ourselves, meaning in our lives that we can only call *soul*. And hopefully you will meet yourself in a very new way, a way you never thought possible.

Again, remember that the soul is not a thing. It is not something that needs to be saved or protected from anything. Nor does it have to follow rules. Because in its essence it is freedom. Rules dam it up, cripple it.

It belongs to you. It *is* you. It's your energy waiting to be used—a way to the power within.

MEANING AND CONNECTION

Let's go back to the basic stuff for a moment—like the cliché that has to be bypassed because it seems so threatening to so many people.

I was sitting in a seminar recently when a middle-aged woman asked the leader: "Can you comment on the meaning of life? It's been bothering me lately."

I couldn't remember the last time I had heard that question asked so unashamedly in public. She was a very brave and honest lady. Because we have to face the fact that these days most everyone is too embarrassed to ask the question out loud, in front of others. We've even become so anxious about it that "Meaning-of-Life" jokes circulate in cycles.

But is there really anyone who doesn't ask the question of themselves, quietly, in private—especially when everything looks useless and bleak and painful? Who is it that doesn't really want to know? If there is anyone alive who doesn't ask the question, then something is terribly wrong.

Yet what *is* the meaning? And how does the discovery of the soul uncover it?

It uncovers it because once the energy begins to move, sensing and seeing connections become inevitable. Connections with everything living. And that is all the meaning there is. *To be and feel fully alive and living.* There isn't any other meaning. And yet it's the most powerful experience there is. It means a *realization* that you are fully alive —and that's all it takes to *be* fully alive.

The first step in seeing this is the last step—because the process is irreversible and it is almost impossible not to go on. Once you are hooked on being alive, you are hooked. Addicted.

Now let's try to get a sense of the vastness of these connections—the connections we can make, because we have them, with everything that lives. Let's produce a scheme, knowing that it is like an incredible blueprint whose lines are all connected, but whose lines you can move and bend at will to create your own final plan, your own creative path, your own fit.

In an amazing book titled *The Reflexive Universe,* Arthur M. Young (who, incidentally, invented the Bell Helicopter) has shown that in the development of the human being, all lesser forms of life—plants, animals, etc. —are contained in some form in the person. The end of it all is nothing more than awareness, consciousness—with a side-by-side growth in the human's ability to have freedom, choice, action, options. But we are still connected to what has gone before us; there is no clean break between plant and animal, animal and person. And Young's heaviest point is that "Each kingdom, and each power, includes what has gone before and adds a contribution of its own. Each kingdom is a level of organization which depends on the one preceding."

What this all says is that everything is connected, everything overlaps, everything is in everything. Because everything that lives, *lives.* There is a similar energy—soul —in everything alive. We are divorced or alienated or separated from nothing because we *can't* be. It isn't possible. We can only *think* we are—and later we'll see how thinking, where it's used improperly, can always give us the idea that we are cut off from what we cannot be cut off from.

We are completely together, completely in touch—except that most of us think we aren't. And we treat that thought-produced fantasy as if it is real.

We have lost nothing. That is why we must come to *recognize* the soul. Because recognize means *to know again.*

And later we will see how it happens in at least one person: we'll see how Mark's relationship to life becomes powerfully released.

We'll see what happens when a person believes that everything is possible.

Come along.

2
Freeing
Your Motion

Everything is possible.

What do we have to lose if we believe that? Seriously: what is there to lose if we believe it? What do *you* lose? The answer is that you can only lose your heaviness, your pessimism, your trap. If you first believe, at least entertain the idea, that everything is possible, then after a period of time you begin to experience that this is so—that everything is really possible. And then you begin to experience the soul.

We like proof, being Western people, and we have a reverence for science that can at times be nothing less than startling—even though the proof comes second, third, or fourth hand. The most enlightened people I know become completely delighted when some personal, intuitive thought is suddenly borne out by a Nobel Prize-winning genius. So be it: that's how we're made in our culture, and we will stay in the pattern until we no longer need it. But let's make an attempt to suspend that rationalism at present. Because here's where excessive rationalism can lead to:

Galileo—who was summoned to the Inquisition in Rome and took that very seriously—at times showed his telescope to the leading sages of the day. The result generally fell into three categories of response. Some were properly struck by what they saw, and some peered around at the other end of the instrument, convinced that Galileo had pasted something on the glass—the picture of a planet, the moon, whatever. But the third group will interest us the most at this point: this group refused to look through the lens. They didn't want to see anything; they didn't want to entertain any possibilities at all. That's how frightened they were. Of what? Of having their old beliefs challenged? Of the truth? What truth?

The same old story again: what they were afraid of was the perception of the *possibility* of truth—whatever that possibility might have been. All you have to do is suggest that possibilities exist—and that seems enough to shake up most people. There seems to be something terribly frightening about possibilities.

Yet they can set you free, they begin to change your life. Immediately. Now.

Ironically, people who believe in the soul as a religious entity—a thing to be saved by certain rules, like the little fellow in the palm of the saint's hand (a pretty far-out idea in and of itself), also can't seem to entertain the thought that the soul is free, is energy. The trouble here is that once you trap something in the form of a material thing, it loses its possibility to be free, to move, to burn, to fly. A declawed or altered cat can no longer roam free outside or mate. It has to stay trapped because something natural that it needs for its wholeness and functioning has been taken from it. Even a plant, removed to a place where it does not belong, no longer has its small freedom to choose the nutrients it needs from a soil that simply won't provide them.

This, of course, is another misuse of materialism. We can't turn anything living into an object without its losing its full meaning.

And if you—a person capable of more freedom than anything else alive—put yourself in a place where the wings of your freedom are clipped, then you too become no more free than the declawed cat or the uprooted plant. Your soul has no room to grow, to use its energy. You damage your freedom by dependency on others—on the rules of a group, of another person, of a whole society if you will. And when you do that, you trap yourself; you become inert; you become a rock, but a fearful one. You lose all mobility by doing what you are told. And worse, accepting it as real, true, that's life, that's the way things are, that's the way it is. And worst of all: you might call it *responsibility*. Playing the game of a responsible person as a way of justifying your lack of mobility and freedom.

Can you begin to sense, just a little, that if we paralyze our mobility, our flow, we dam up our energy, our radiance, and our fingers begin to slip away from the soul that belongs to us?

An example: something that had never before happened in my practice.

A woman in her middle fifties came to see me on the advice of her daughter whom I had been able to help some years before. She was a very attractive woman in every way, but her face was incredibly pained, pinched, and her mouth was drawn down in a look of perpetual bitterness. I asked her what was wrong.

"I know what my problem is. I'm enraged. I'm so enraged that I can't eat, I can't talk to anyone any more, I can hardly sleep. And when I do sleep I dream of rage. I'm a murderer in my dreams. There isn't a thing I haven't killed or tried to kill in my dreams. I've destroyed whole cities in my dreams. Worse than Hiroshima."

And in waking life?

"I'd like to kill everybody who jams the subways. . . . window-shoppers. . . . I'd like a machinegun. . . ."

With that, the fingers of her right hand, which had been playing nervously with the worn fabric on the arm of her chair, tore through it, ripping away a swatch several inches long. She began to cry, trying to wedge the material back in place, pressing it down.

All I could do was ask her what she was angry about. It was feeble, but I couldn't think of anything else to say.

"All my life those bastards have told me what to do, and now, just like that"—she tried to snap her fingers but they were too agitated to do anything but rub soundlessly—"they changed the rules on me and it's all been for nothing. I've given up my whole damn life for nothing—just to have them. . . ." She gagged.

"Who's *they*?"

"The Church, that's who."

I had never heard anything like this. Anger usually involves a person, a group, even something you can't put your finger on. But the Church?

She saw it this way:

"I've done everything according to the laws of the Church. Six children because I couldn't use any kind of birth control and rhythm never worked for me. I've done what my husband wanted because he's the man. I've confessed all my sins and never ate meat on Friday and went to Mass every Sunday, and obeyed all the Commandments. Whenever I got mad at my mother or father I confessed it. And maybe the worst of it all was that I could have gone to college, used my brain—I'm not a stupid woman. But I had my first baby at twenty, and that was that.

"Why am I mad? I'm mad because I've lived all of my life believing that the Church was the truth, that the laws God gave to man were *forever*. That all the laws were unchangeable—the way I said—forever. And then overnight they changed them like nothing they ever said mattered. You know, there's a church on Long Island that keeps the Mass in Latin, and I went there for a while, but it didn't work."

She stared at me and in a measured, almost doomstruck voice, said:

"I ruined my life. And now it's too late to do anything about it."

It took a long while for her to realize that it wasn't too late. That she was trapped in the past. That she had to focus on the Now that she had let slip past her life—and maybe the most difficult thing for her to accept was that she had given herself up to something outside of herself, willingly. Before she could move into her own self-discovery she had to take responsibility for that. She had to see possibilities. She had to ignite her soul so that she could move.

But the most poignant example of this abdication of the soul, of the deadening of its energy, occurred in an orthodox Jewish woman I learned of through her brother. She told her husband that she could no longer tolerate her role—that she felt stifled and dead. Instead of finding out what she meant, there followed a whole procession of family members telling her what to do, how to live and act. Whereupon she began to withdraw, no longer going out because she had no one to talk to, to understand her, until one day her husband came home from work and found her hidden away, pressed flat, under their bed, silent and motionless. A paradox: to avoid her trap, to leave it, she retreated into a dark hidden place, like a sick animal in a zoo. She spent a long time in a mental hospital where every effort to get her to move outward drove her deeper into silence, into a tight little pocket. According to her brother, the first words she said in response to a nurse after months of silence raised the hair on everyone's necks. Quoting Martin Luther King's epitaph, she looked up at the nurse and said:

"Free at last, free at last. Thank God Almighty, I'm free at last."

DEEPENING TRAPS

We often deepen our traps in efforts to leave them. And it *is* a paradox—often a terribly painful one. First, we have a tendency to believe that the traps we find ourselves in are all created and maintained by external circumstances or realities—like jails. We often seem to have very little sense that we have largely created the traps: if we developed this sense, we would clearly see that whatever we've gotten ourselves into, we can get ourselves out of.

But there always seems to be some point of no return at which we think that we are completely helpless, victims of circumstance. We lose sight of all possibilities and see everything controlled by social forces and our own guilt.

The fact we least want to believe is that we have set our own traps—and then promptly spring them. Yet this realization is the only means by which we can set ourselves free. Part of our denial of all this is that the truth we must face about our traps must by definition lead to a terribly frightening awareness—frightening, that is, for most of us.

Because I have never met a person who didn't feel trapped by social, religious, or economic demands.

EXPLORATION: Think of all the ways in which you feel trapped, situations you feel you can't leave. See them, define them for yourself. Is there even *one* that *isn't* rooted into some form of social demand?

This realization has to get at you—and get at you deeply. It implies that the rules may be crazy—not your desire for freedom. That many of the social goals we have worked to attain may well be illusions, even meaningless. Else why would we feel trapped?

We achieve the great dream, buy our houses in the suburbs, and find ourselves needing to make more money, find ourselves depressed from getting exactly "what we wanted." Lovers marry, then in a decade become a divorce statistic. You can go on and on with this—and become more and more depressed.

We trap ourselves by thinking, at first believing, that we can find happiness, meaning, and fulfillment by identifying ourselves with the whole social game.

Friends of mine, a young childless couple, spontaneously bought a house simply because they wanted one. Nobody seems to be able to understand why they bought the house. Why a house? They don't have kids. She must be pregnant. (She isn't.) Or maybe she's barren. Is he sterile?

They don't fit the "normal" pattern. They're different. And nobody seems to want to see *that*.

It makes you wonder if some people have children

in order to justify buying a house. Or buy a house in order to justify having children.

When we play by these rules, we set our traps. When we refuse to recognize that the rules are worthless, we deepen our traps. We deepen our traps every time we avoid the possibility of taking our freedom by doing something individual. We deepen them every time we play a social game.

But we deepen them even more dramatically when we don't take responsibility for what we are, when we try hard to convince ourselves that we can't move.

EXPLORATION: Re-examine the traps. Focus very hard on the idea that you have set them, sprung them. *See* this and you will understand that you can set yourself free. Get used to the idea that you set the trap by your lack of awareness, your lack of a full connection with yourself— so that all of your knowledge, intuition, and feeling were not working together. And ultimately awareness will free you. *Nothing else can.*

Again, our tremendous dependency is at work here— and never forget that we human beings, because of our incredibly drawn-out childhoods, have dependency woven deeply into our basic fabric—and oftentimes the harder we attempt to work our way out of our traps the more frightened we become because freedom seems to mean being utterly, totally, alone and cut off from the people, the groups, the rules we *think* give us protection and meaning.

To be free is to be an adult—and to be truly an adult, free.

And no amount of lip-service to the idea of "responsibility" makes a person an adult.

Freedom *is* responsibility.

The lack of it brings people into psychotherapy.

And the most dependent people are those who think they have no problems, those who "know" how to live.

Yet in what I've just said is a key to the door. Most people who come to therapy, in general all people who see the task of life as one of acquiring self-knowledge, realize that the way out of their traps must lie in directions different from the ones they have tried in the past. They have come to see, sometimes after intense pain, that they cannot think their way out of an emotional dilemma. That the rules they have learned provide no path to freedom or meaning except as defined by the rules themselves.

"I love the law," a young law student proudly said at a party. "If you work within the law, all sorts of social changes are possible."

To which an old writer responded:

"Change is possible only when the law is *broken*."

He was not advocating anarchy.

So we deepen our traps by attempting to find solutions within the rules, within the "law." And that is the wrong place.

We must look in a different direction.

And the direction is inward, where the real possibilities are, where the movement goes on endlessly, ceaselessly. We can only hurt ourselves if we try to stop it.

CHANGING THE ORDER

So suppose I repeat to you that everything is possible. That finding your freedom and your soul means letting go of old useless ways. Letting your own motion take over. We can begin with a simple exercise.

EXPLORATION: Most of us have a defined morning

ritual before we finally get out of the house to go to work. In some rigid order which we haven't consciously planned, but which has taken us over, we might do the following: leave the bed, go to the bathroom, put on the coffee, shave or shower, go back and pour the coffee, drink some, return to the bedroom, begin to dress, have some more of the coffee, glance at the paper if we have it delivered, then leave.

Find out what your order is. Then one morning change it. Vary the routine. Do it backwards, any way at all, so long as it's different. *Don't think it through. Do it.* Then see what you feel.

Unless we are completely unconscious, we will feel a little anxious, a little confused, a little unnerved, a little exhilarated, or some combination of all. We will have a sense of having done something very different, and we will sense that even in the smallest things, the smallest unconscious routine, we can feel nervous if we take our freedom by the act of changing something, of changing a pattern.

Try it or you won't feel anything. Get used to the sense that day after day, on the most apparently insignificant level, we behave like that group of "sages" who refused to look through Galileo's telescope because they might *see* something.

An exploration like this (did you feel yourself resisting? wanting to do it?) can begin to prep you for major surgery that can help lay bare the soul. Except that you have to try it; without the try you will never know that the routine traps you—and that is the most dangerous kind of unconsciousness.

EXPLORATION: On a less physical level, but very dynamic. The next time you're having a conversation with someone and it turns into a debate over what is really a minor issue, see that your debate develops from having turned something ostensibly unimportant into a vaguely life-or-death issue. A fight occurs; you are defensive; something inside of you is being challenged. But what?

Now this will take, at least at first, a great effort of will—but *bow out of the quarrel.* Say out loud, or even to yourself: "This fight is taking place because one of us isn't seeing something clearly. That one of us, that somebody, may be me." Then listen to the other person. See if you can just listen. And if you can, see if you can listen without beginning to form a counterargument. See if you can just, pure and simple, listen to what's being said.

It will be very difficult. Because what has been happening is that you've been engaged in a battle in which you have not been seeing the other person at all. You've not been seeing yourself, either. You've been only defending yourself against some kind of "attack." And the chances are, it's all in the mind—that what you're fighting about is something you don't *know* through your experience. Because if you *know,* a fight isn't possible; if you *think* you know, if you believe without experience, then the fight takes place.

Like the morning-routine exercise, bowing out might make you nervous, especially if you're a man. (Men are supposed to punch and counterpunch.) But you will see something about yourself.

We find this sort of thing threatening because there is always the possibility that the other person may be Galileo's telescope. Not a fact, but simply a possibility.

All this puts the burden on you. But isn't that as it should be? Isn't that where it belongs? We aren't going to discover anything about ourselves unless we assume the responsibility for what we do and feel. You can't unstick yourself painlessly.

The master key is to try things in different ways, and the main lesson right now is to see, to understand, how difficult it is, how painful it might be. That's all—the first step. Just to understand how hard it can be, to get some sense of that. And knowing that, feeling it from your own experience, makes it easier to get on with it.

DEMOLISHING SKEPTICISM

Here's where it's important to demolish skepticism, because skepticism is one of the most prevalent and damaging counterforces to recognizing the power of the soul, a short-circuit *par excellence* of inner energy. It prevents a living connection, and so it keeps us deadened, inert, checks our every movement.

The problem with skepticism is that it has become an accepted *position*. It is even supposed to label a person "smart." *But skepticism is total passivity: you don't have to do, feel, or think anything at all to be a skeptic.* All you have to do is say *No*. You just have to be negative. It's an uncharged position, like a dead battery; it has no life to it. It's a wall trying to dam up a flow.

The "position" is accepted because it comes from the *misuse* and *misunderstanding* of the scientific viewpoint which for decades has had us by the throats. It's a show-me position that takes the place of imagination with as deadly an effect as a surgical brain transplant.

But why should anyone *show* me anything? Why should anyone have to *prove* anything to me?

Skepticism is a position of arrogance—and it is utterly

devoid of imagination and creativity. No spontaneity at all. Yet how can such total passivity be so arrogant? Precisely because anything so passive, so inert, so without curiosity and a sense of wonder, finds itself cut off from its own energy—and so it lives in a world of being acted upon by forces outside itself, and in its helplessness it becomes arrogant. Helplessness—then it feels fear and becomes a dictator that persecutes anything new and different. In psychology this process is called "overcompensation." But kids peg it in a different way: inside every bully is a coward. The skeptic hurts himself far more than he can ever hurt you.

Maybe at this point you might be asking: what about the "healthy" skeptic? The person who isn't in the habit of buying the Brooklyn Bridge or getting set up by con men? The "healthy" skeptic hangs loose. The healthy skeptic doesn't believe everything he hears—but what he does is investigate. Not with the idea of disproving something, but with the idea of finding something that may enrich him. Implicit in the healthy skeptic is that he might find something, and so he sets off actively. He seeks experience. Openly. And so he is not really a skeptic at all. He just wants to do it *himself.*

Suppose we glance back at the last two Explorations. The true skeptic will not try either of them, the main reason being that someone has suggested them to him. He will call it all nonsense. But how can he know it is anything at all unless he tries? Obviously he won't try, so therefore he knows nothing. Or he will try only to defeat the purpose.

It is important for the skeptic that nothing ever happens.

So we can say, with pretty good assurance, that the

skeptic keeps himself deliberately in ignorance, in his dark trap. This idea is crucial for almost all that follows. *Skepticism is a position of inert, self-willed ignorance. It is soulless.*

The "healthy" skeptic, if you want to use that term, *will* try—with the idea of experiencing something. And that is a position of self-willed *knowledge.*

Now it might have occurred to you that I've left out the people who, seeming not to be skeptical at all, still won't try anything—anything at all. That may be because in some profound way they don't take their lives seriously. But that is another story. Let's put it off for a while.

EXPLORATION: First let's see if we can loosen up our heads right now—entertain a few possibilities. Things we might never have thought could happen—but have happened and do happen. Let's try to sense if we get uneasy about them; excited by them; even uncaring. Do they have any meaning for our lives, inner and outer?

• Findhorn. A community in Scotland located on a barren North Sea peninsula where even in the cold of winter huge brilliantly colored flowers grow in sandy, gravelly soil that is not supposed to support any vegetation but scrubby stunted pines and scrawny radishes. They have also grown cabbages there weighing over forty pounds—and countless other mammoth vegetables. Visitors are overwhelmed with feelings of love; they hear buzzes and see glows. Peter Caddy, Findhorn's founder, describes the place as a "cosmic power point." He and his wife ask for things and they seem to materialize: they need concrete for a wall and bags of cement drop off a passing truck. This happens all the time. The reports are all consistent. The Findhorners say they communicate with nature spirits; they want to grow not just big vegetables, but great people.

In the concrete scientific framework of our day, no one can quite figure out how they do it.

• In Tibet, before the Chinese takeover, many witnesses saw such things as men possessed by "spirits" who could lean their eyes against the points of swords—as in India you can still see *fakirs* sitting in a trance on beds of spikes, or walking calmly through banks of hot coals. But the most spectacular of all are the men who loped through the wilds of Tibet, through all but impassable terrain, lightly clothed in the freezing cold, and with eyes closed or staring at some point in the sky—traveling completely surefooted without a single mishap. These men could move at the speed of ten miles per hour—and cover distances of 300 miles without resting. Not even the best of our athletes, in top shape and on the best of roads, could match them.

• By a process called "cloning," you can grow a whole frog by regenerating cells taken from a single part of the original body.

• People have been able to wire a plant to a polygraph (the common lie detector) and get strong "panicky" electric readings not only when an animal or another plant is harmed nearby, but even when bacteria are killed in a sink by scalding water. Plants seem to react "negatively" when live organisms are damaged. One man detected the same adverse reaction in his wired plant when he destroyed the bacteria in his yogurt while spooning in jam loaded with chemical colors and preservatives. Another man, when confronted with an ailing plant, can enter a meditation-like state, visualize himself entering the plant, and find the exact location of the damage. Both blood and cell scrapings from human beings will react in the same way in response to "sensing" harm to living things.

Are we beginning to sense the idea of *connection*

here? People with plants, people with the whole environment? Living things with themselves?

• A woman client of mine who has always liked nature, but only as an observer, enters a deep state of inner visualization, images herself as a bird, and sees herself for the first time as *part* of nature and not just as an onlooker. She crosses the gulf of the observer-object split. She is able now to do this in the outside world; she can lose all meaning of time while being deliberately involved with the stars, and emerges from the experience renewed, fresh, filled with energy. Materially, she is *very, very* successful. She is no "mystic" in the spiritual marketplace.

• Another client, always afraid of death, gains the courage to face it within. She speaks to death, asks it questions. Death tells her exactly what its function is. She feels it, sees it, keeps experiencing it—and with time her fear begins to ebb. She begins to see death as a part of the *process* of life and not some meaningless termination of it. Also no mystic. And she has a thriving, practical career.

• A man I know meets a "clairvoyant" woman at a party. They talk. He then has two obviously predictive dreams. He links their occurrence to the brief encounter with the woman, but also realizes that if he had paid any attention to his dreams, such experiences might not be rare at all.

And are we also beginning to sense that to make these connections a different way of seeing is necessary? Not of thinking, but of *seeing*. Of seeing the possibilities.

You as well as I could add a great many examples to such a list. But I've saved my best one for last, because it makes a point of the utmost importance.

GETTING AROUND THE RULES

The biologist Lyall Watson—and he is as hard-nosed a scientist as they come—was witness to an incredible demonstration by a group of people in Toronto. These people wanted to see if they could produce a group hallucination by conjuring up a ghost—but the fresh twist was that the ghost was not to be a manifestation of a "real" dead person. Instead they literally invented him: a seventeenth-century nobleman they called Philip, with a completely fictional biography. They tried for two unsuccessful years to conjure up the imaginary Philip, then at one of their meetings they began spontaneously to horse around, cavorting like children—and suddenly the table began to rock. Today, while the group still hasn't seen Philip, they can produce his presence by fooling around like children, singing childish songs—in general letting go of their usual adult façades. Let's let Watson tell it:

> While I sat with the Philip group one evening they became involved with a long and splendidly bawdy conversation with their imagined ghost, who ended the session by lifting a very heavy table until all four legs were off the ground and pursuing the photographer from an American magazine round the room with it until it had him pinned to a wall.

And in stressing that the production of Philip was largely due to the group's spontaneous child-like behavior, free of normal adult constraints and rules, he adds:

But what they have shown is that any group of people, ordinary folk without a single psychic pretension among them, can produce, on demand and at will, well-developed paranormal phenomena. *Anyone can get round the rules of traditional science simply by pretending they don't exist.* (My emphasis.)

Let's get around the rules. The way to the soul is not through science or through set rules and attitudes—and as Watson implies by example, getting "round" science can also be fun. And the other point we will be stressing as we go on is precisely the idea that it is the in-touchness with the child within that revives and nourishes the growth of the soul. Because children *really* have soul—until it is wrenched from them by forcing them into an upbringing geared to "real life" at the expense of the inner world and the imagination.

And right here we might as well redefine "paranormal." It is neither strange, eerie, otherworldly, bizarre, or any other freak-show or horror-movie term. It is simply seeing in a different way and liberating energy that has been bottled up in "adult" pursuits that instead of enhancing our capacity to experience, have significantly damaged them.

It is completely ordinary. We just have to retrain ourselves, get it back, absorb the possibility that it's there. To do it requires spontaneity, the vision of a child —which we *can* have while being adult, although we tend to think that once we enter adulthood we are no longer children—a falsehood, and a dangerous one. If we had stayed connected to all levels of our development we would have lost nothing—including the incredible curiosity of a child before he becomes specialized. A curiosity that is all beautiful and connected to everything—a soul that can identify itself with everything within and without. And not having to name or think it away.

For example, most of us have had the experience of seeing some object from a new perspective. We might be sitting and reading, then pause and look up from our book. And there is this object that we can't identify. Our immediate reaction is to get up and examine it: "Oh, a pencil, a leaf fallen from a plant—that's what it is!" In quiet terms, this is almost a "Thank God it's only a pencil" response. We *have* to name it, identify it; otherwise we become nervous. A child would just look.

And that's what "paranormal" is all about. Permitting ourselves to see things from new angles of perception.

That's all it takes: to return to a state of childhood, of pure sight, in which all forces are seen and felt and experienced as new. A world in which animals and inanimate objects have lives of their own and are magical and can think and speak. Really.

If you have trouble with that, look at your cat or dog. You attribute intent and meaning to it always. You see it doing what it does deliberately, with purpose. You are sure it thinks. You feel it can be just as loving or just as nasty as any person—*willingly and with intention.*

If you didn't, your pet wouldn't be in the house. Why would you want a dumb piece of flesh and hair hanging around? And wonder about this: if we attribute all these "so-called" human traits to our animals, we might, just possibly, be right.

Who can tell *you* differently? You connect with your animal, and that's what it's all about. In terms of the soul, of human connection, what on earth would be the point of a scientific refutation—even if it could be made? Would we quickly get rid of our pets?

With people, though, this is different—but that is because as adults we are tight and defensive with each other, and we will be going very deeply into that because it's a position we have to free ourselves from in order to get back to the basics. Keep in mind that with animals we somehow manage to get back to some in-touchness with the freshness of childhood. And that is all the difference in the world. It's entirely possible that that's why we keep animals in the first place—to see a hidden side of ourselves.

EXPLORATION: If you have an animal, make eye-contact with it and hold a conversation. In very human terms, describe the animal to itself, tell it what it's like. Tell it what you think of it, tell it everything you can about it—positive, negative, everything. *But put it all on a human level, using only human attributes.* Throw "objectivity" to the wind. See the animal as human.

Now you've just described *yourself*—or a lot about yourself.

If your description has matched what you think and feel about yourself, there's a nice comfortable "fit." But if there's a difference, a discrepancy, large or small, you're putting onto your animal a number of your own qualities, feelings, or thoughts of which you are not aware, are out of touch with.

Bad or good, see that these qualities are yours, *inside you*. If you see the animal as warm, then there's warmth inside *you*. If you see the animal as having few wants, then somewhere inside you is a person who wishes to have a simpler life. And so on.

This exploration is extremely effective, and you can even do it at a zoo with any animal of your choice.

Now proceed a step further.

EXPLORATION: Look at yourself in a mirror, preferably one that limits itself to the image of your face—like a large hand mirror.

Contact your eyes, hold them, and begin to describe the person before you—the way you did with the animal. When you're finished, just keep the eye contact going. Keep looking. Focus, concentrate.

Do this for as long as you can take it.

Do it every day for a month.

And just watch, just *see*, what happens in the mirror.

THE MYTH OF OBJECTIVITY

So in keeping with the Explorations, let's end this chapter with a major poke at another scientific sacred cow—which by all means we must, as Watson says, get "round." And that is the myth of objectivity, that says, in one way, that things and people can act or behave or respond completely free of the intervention of another human being. Or put in another way, things or people can behave according to fixed laws that have nothing to do with *me*.

That may be true when an electrically activated hammer hits an object which then breaks a piece of glass. And it will do that every time if the same constant charge is applied to the hammer. That is mechanics, and it has to do with inert things. (The skeptic, the pessimist, operates mechanically because he is inert: we can always predict what he will do when confronted with something new or different.) But we are interested in movement, because everything alive has this potentiality.

Mechanics has nothing to do with people.

Nor with animals.

Nor plants.

Nor perhaps the whole connected universe.

It is not even true of atomic particles—and the breakthrough here was made by a Nobel Laureate, Werner Heisenberg, who turned the scientific world on its tail when he demonstrated that simply by the act of observing something you change or affect that something's properties.

This is especially so with people. We have never seen a person *alone* in the privacy of his own territory—when he is completely alone, visible to no one. We are all connected, but the connection is observable only when we meet face-to-face. And then nothing can be objective. Even if you spy on someone, the *intention* in your spying makes the scene nonobjective. Your *reason* is spying—and that reason will color what you observe. For good or ill, there is no objectivity. It can mostly be good.

Let's keep that in mind because it will take us straight into ourselves in a very living way.

"Objectivity," incidentally, is a way in which we avoid responsibility for ourselves—our thoughts and actions. We blame others for many of our misfortunes—because "everybody knows that guy is a mean bastard"— or some such.

And the term, the concept, has tried to work its way into psychotherapy, with, I might add, absolutely no success. Very often people who come for consultation say to the therapist: "I'd like someone to look at my problems objectively."

Since the therapist is human, it can't be done.

Otherwise there would be no one looking.

3
The Inside-
Outside "Split"

What corrodes possibilities? What knocks them out of us early in our lives like a short circuit in a complex electrical system?

The answer always seems to return to the same place: the exaggerated emphasis on materialism. The *over-emphasis.*

By materialism I don't mean exclusively money or possessions—although these are very important factors that can work powerfully against the exercise of courage and the development of the inner freedom of the soul. For example, the person who simply "can't" develop himself or herself because these is a house to support, bills to pay, children to care for, etc., *ad infinitum.*

But materialism is far more subtle than that because, being deep inside us, we being encouraged to embrace it early in life, it invades every part of our existence and clings to our thoughts as napalm clings to the skin. It some-times seems impossible to get rid of its hold on us.

The simplest example in the world, something every-one seems to have experienced: you can't sleep; you may even have what you feel like calling chronic insomnia. You toss and turn because something plagues your mind; thoughts come fast and furious, usually some worry—a worry, I should add, that has to do with something ma-terial, something you did or didn't do. Maybe you don't want to dream because you don't want to know some-thing that is beginning to emerge from within you.

If this persists you go to the doctor and, often without the slightest inquiry into what might *really* be bothering you, he will prescribe Valium (perhaps addictive) or some sleeping potion like Seconal. It is common knowledge that a doctor who knows nothing about what makes your psyche tick can legally prescribe anything he wants. Even your dentist can prescribe Valium.

What we have accepted here, as soon as we accept the prescription and begin to pop the pills, is pure mater-ialism.

Because this particular doctrine of materialism states that we, as human beings, have no power, no way of handling our own upsets—and ultimately have no soul. It states that only what we can *buy* has the power to help us.

We need a pill. That will fix us up. That will fix every-body up. It will also expand the assets of drug companies. A sort of spiral begins here: we may even hold stock in a drug company that pays us some sort of inconsequential dividend precisely because we can't sleep and we buy the company's product.

But the selling point is: we can't do anything about

our sleeplessness. It isn't ours to examine, cope with, and end. We need that pill. *We need something from the outside.* Something with clout. A power. In this case, a drug. And we are supposed to believe it—believe *in* it.

Except that if you believe in the power of the pill, I can give you a placebo—a pill containing nothing but chalk or some other powerless substance—and you will also, chances are, fall asleep if I tell you that I have given you the real thing.

The real thing may work because it has chemical properties that relax or knock you out. The placebo will work because you believe it's real—you believe *in* it. This is the religion of materialism. You get hooked on an illusion and believe it's real. This sort of materialism relies completely on our dependency and our gullibility.

But there *are no illusions* deep inside us. All we have to do, if we can see some air outside the mound of pills and worries, is to readjust our perception of our sleeplessness. What we are probably sleepless about is partly the anxiety of not being able to sleep: I will be tired in the morning; I need eight hours of sleep to function (do I really?); it's *bad* not to sleep.

EXPLORATION: If you are sleepless, just get up. Pour a glass of milk, a glass of wine, taste it, drink it, read a book you've been putting off; do a jigsaw puzzle, needlepoint. Or take advantage of your aloneness, close your eyes, and look inside instead of at the clock. Do the thing your body has been trying to tell you to do: get up. But if you want to keep it a problem, make sure you walk around like a zombie the next day, or goof something up, in order to prove that you need the sleep. Like the business executive who fogs through an afternoon's work after a liquid lunch and blames it all on his lack of sleep the night before.

Begin to see the possibility that you might need nothing outside of yourself to regulate your own pace. *See what keeps you sleepless.* See if you really believe what you're anxious about—or if it's something you've read or been told.

If you believe in the possibilities of a pill—which, again, may have the same effect as a dot of chalk, why not believe in the possibilities that you can do the job yourself?

GAUGUIN'S REVELATION

When I think of our incredible reliance on the outside, I invariably think of Paul Gauguin who left the sterility of his European environment to find freedom, bliss, and subject matter to paint in the tropical islands. He thought he would find the "noble savage" in a natural setting. Instead he found total colonization and a world fast becoming plastic. His agony was profound.

But at some point in time, he turned inward and began to paint what was inside him, what always existed inside him. And *that's* the Gauguin we know, the Gauguin we call great. All those landscapes, those magnificent sensual women in their Polynesian *sarongs:* they never existed in the world around him. They were products of his creative imagination.

Difficult to grasp—but true.

In a way, that is the whole thrust of the modern humanistic techniques of therapy as well as the current emphasis on meditation. *Get in touch with your possibilities.* This is an emphasis on the human being's movement and growth—not on his "sickness," but on what he puts in the way of his own movement.

Getting up and having a drink or a read is practical. Mark, the young man you met at the beginning, had a similar problem that reaped him more dividends than simply ending his sleeplessness. It wasn't that he couldn't get to sleep, it was that he would wake anywhere from five to six in the morning—but with all the same anxieties about sleeplessness. He began to read—not work—and then after several weeks he began to become aware of his body, then more of his self.

> I started to see that it was a very beautiful time of day. Dark, but not *hard* dark like a night out in the city. Soft dark. The air is soft, quiet, somehow very sweet. The world seems to be yours. I began to be very aware that I was sitting in the chair; tossing around in bed I was just aware of my thoughts, my head going around in circles. But in the chair, in all that soft light, I felt myself *being* there. I guess this would sound silly to a lot of people, but I know I have hair on my arms, right? I mean everybody sort of *knows* that. But I became aware one night that I have *hairs* on my arms. I don't suppose that would mean much to anyone, just the telling of it—Hey, Oh wow, I have *hairs* on my arms. But what a sensation it was! It was like suddenly not taking for granted something about my own body.

And there was a woman who made one of the most dramatic, yet easiest, flows from feeling herself to be a sick—physically sick—person, into a picture of herself as not sick at all—just afraid of being sick. She had visited a lot of doctors, all of whom kept her in a constant state of ambiguity, suspense, and despair—while her own anxiety prevented her from asking meaningful, pointed questions. A possible "growth" in her breast might or might not be malignant; in fact there might or might not have been a growth at all. Her sense of losing her hearing might be caused by damage to the nervous system; or it might not; maybe it was wax; maybe there was *nothing* wrong. Maybe—in the favorite terminology of many physicians—she was just a "crock," which is an unkind word for a hypochondriac.

Yet nowhere in this woman's dreams or in her visualizations with me was there the slightest trace that she felt herself deeply to be a sick person.

And that's all I pointed out to her—and she was immediately able to recognize that sickness was an idea that had come at her from the outside via her parents and colleagues, but that inside she was not at all burdened by a self-image of being sick. As a matter of fact she could be quite carefree and connected.

But back to Mark. One early morning he was sitting, no longer reading, his eyes loosely fixed on a plant, a palm.

It turned pink, softly graduated to pinkish-purple. And then it blazed a glowing red.

He did something then that is crucial if we want to see differently: he didn't turn away or try to account for what was happening. He simply trained in on the plant. And was overwhelmed by the magic of it.

A red palm.

And then the red began to fade away; and soon the room was filled with sunlight.

What he had seen was the rising sun catching the

palm in its light, but the later realization of what had happened didn't diminish the experience of seeing a piece of magic unfold before his eyes. Instead, it turned his thoughts for the first time in years back to school, to a mythology course he had taken. The experience of the palm recalled for him some of the myths in which the sun was believed to be alive, the magical power of life and energy, the source of everything on earth.

It also opened up something else for him, almost the first step in his understanding of *how* his soul was not generating, was cut off.

> It didn't hit me until later in the day, when I got a phone call from the man I usually share the beach house with. It struck me that I've spent summer after summer there—right on the water facing east—and not once had I ever seen a sunrise. It was right there, the sun, coming up every morning, and never once did I get up early enough to see it.
>
> And I thought: My God, if it can do something like that in a room in the middle of the city—lighting up a plant that way—what must it be like watching it while you're standing on the beach, watching what it does to the surf, the water, the sand—what it does to you? It could turn me red! It could light me up.
>
> I got very sad—not depressed, just sad. I looked back at all those years with a powerful feeling that I had missed something incredible. That it was right there and I had never looked at it once. I don't think I ever missed a human being as much.

The implications of that last line were not to unfold for him for some time: "I don't think I ever missed a human being as much." Recall what he said earlier—that he was surrounded by things, that women were things, that he himself was a thing broken into fragments.

Of course he could never have missed a person as much; people were never quite real for him, important enough. He connected as little with them as he connected with the sun which every summer rose on his doorstep begging for notice. All of which means, in his own words really, that he was disconnected from himself—"Like I don't have a soul."

He was never quite real to himself, not really important to himself, not taking his life seriously. Despite his success with business and money and all the rest.

TAKING LIFE SERIOUSLY

To take our lives seriously we have to be in touch with something big, something great, wondrous, and immense within ourselves. Otherwise life is little, material, drained of magic, insignificant, and isolated—disconnected, the fragments he talked of. The big connection must be made. Or it all stays small, painful, meaningless—and then we begin to think of wasted lives, of wishing to leave something to posterity, of wishing to be seen and recognized. We begin to be afraid of death (children are curious, but not afraid of it) because we have a sense that we haven't lived.

Pieces, parts, fragments, disconnection: hear the language, see in your mind's eye a universe banging and zooming around, every piece seeming to have no sense to it—people slamming out at you from doorways and elevators, cars screeching, sirens wailing. Nothing working down here because nothing connected in a way we can understand. *Listen* to the noises. Literally listen.

What was beginning to happen to Mark was that he was glimpsing where he fit—not fit like a cog in a machine, a worker on an assembly line, or any of that. He began to see where he fit into *meaning*—and that without the fit he was a fragment flying about with no sense to him, no depth—and more, that he was fragmented inside and so was not "working," was not bound by the energy of his soul. And this is important.

Because as Arthur Young of *The Reflexive Universe* puts it: *The whole is greater than the sum of its parts.*

Except we were never taught that; more, any sense we might have had of it was knocked out of us. Because if you want to make a human being into a cog that works for you, buys your products, follows your rules, and keeps in line—you have to show him that he is not whole. And a very good way to do this is to "educate" people as if they are objects, things, or concepts. Like in plane geometry, where the whole can *only* be *equal* to the sum of its parts. But as humans we are not comprised of angles, curves, or chunks of flat space divided by straight lines.

As a client of mine remarked: "Today I began to talk about specific little goals—and then I realized that the more I went on, the more I looked beneath them, I was opening up the whole universe."

That's what it's there for.

With people, the whole must be greater than the sum of its parts because we move, do, get from one place to another physically and emotionally—in short we function entirely *as* a whole, even if sometimes it doesn't feel that way. Your detached leg won't go anywhere by itself without your will behind it; even less can it take you anywhere at all if there is no rest of you to take anywhere. Your eyes, cut from their nerves and placed on a table, see nothing.

Sad to say, our eyes *have* been cut—and they will stay cut if all we can do with them is see the same old things in the same old ways.

I have heard of an old man who walks in the woods and sees gnomes cavorting, and little wood spirits, and a number of times he has seen the nature god Pan. He finds it all very beautiful and meaningful.

The cut eyes on the table "see" the man, but not *what* he sees; and our well-trained mouths may say: "He's crazy!" Suppose he isn't? Suppose he is happy, peaceful, has been materially successful, feels his fit in the universe, is never destructive toward others, has a mind which, sharp as a tack, can trade off in a "logical" argument point by point, can be oriented to *everyday* reality any time he chooses— with as equal an ease as he can meet with his forest people?

How would the eyes on the table see him then? What would the mouth say? He is *partly* crazy?

Let's weigh this: to accept that he is all this is to discover possibilities. To deny anything has no purpose whatever—except to close doors on the possibilities.

Now. Suppose the disconnected eyes were able to see not just the man himself but also what he sees on his morning walks: a fat little gnome, the image of Pan with his horns and cloven hooves, carrying his pipes.

Like as not, a great tragedy would occur. The mouth would probably say: "*I'm* crazy!" But this would be a conditioned reaction: because if the eyes *could* see what the old man sees, we would be functioning as a whole and craziness would not be a concept at all. We would just be a little shaken at first—before we trusted our ability to experience.

Incidentally, most "bad" LSD trips are not "bad" because the images that emerge from within are frightening *per se*. They are frightening largely because they are totally, utterly unfamiliar to us. They are there, inside, like Gauguin's creations; it is just that we have had no experience with them—and being strange to us, we "naturally" consider them enemies.

To clarify, I am not saying that with a little practice we are all going out on a field trip to frolic with wood nymphs. I am just saying that the possibility exists that we might be able to. (Actually I'll suggest later how you can get part of the way there—to wood nymphs, or whatever else there is inside of *you* individually. And I will show you how a whole society has done it.)

For now, remember the point and its intuitive sense: the soul is not material and neither are possibilities. In fact possibilities threaten materialism. So that possibilities and the soul have something deeply in common.

The eyes must get back into the whole or they won't function *as* a whole.

THE LOSS OF SEEING

Damaging the soul by losing the ability to see starts with a misconception—that parenting and education must pivot on the "fact" that children, who are later to be adults, need to be educated exclusively in a way that gives them tools to work and make it in the practical material world. Of course this is true—so far as it goes. But the idea is totally misbalanced because that's what our education *limits* itself to. Education also tacitly assumes that children are happiest when conforming and unhappiest when "different." But this is a vicious circle because most systems of education *create* the rules and standards, and pressure the different child to conform—and if he or she doesn't, the boom of criticism is lowered. So obviously the nonconforming child will be unhappy.

Our education completely neglects the inner vision, the spiritual needs of a human being: it gears him only to the practical and material at the expense of everything else. One result is a feeling we've all had: when we think of radical self-change, we think of losing financial and social security—and possibilities become fearfully blocked off.

Usually nonmaterial needs have been handled in the past by such activities as keeping the Sabbath holy, and I remember very clearly the pastor of my childhood church (circa 1941) giving one hell of a brimstone sermon about working on Sundays. He talked of greed, avarice, materialism, until I got anxious on the spot the next time I saw my father trim hedges on a Sunday morning. He, the clippers, the hedges—all something taking place in the devil's workshop.

Anyway, as Archie and Edith Bunker would croon it, "Those were the days." And it was mixed up anyway, because the same pastor, on Sunday morning, could also call for a third collection because something or other needed to be built or bought, and add: "And I don't want to hear any jingling in the baskets." Only the crinkle of bills. He saw no inconsistency in any of this: his split between the inner life and outer "necessity" was complete. Leading a spiritual flock and needing to pay the bills is a difficult position to begin with.

Bear in mind, again, a very critical, a core, concept: that the materialistic orientation becomes so ingrained only because of its misbalance, because of the idea that *all things in life seem derived from it.* Note the *seem.* Happiness, self-esteem, meaning, integrity, status, etc., etc. In one way or another, you're supposed to be able to "buy" them all.

But if you haven't got these things inside you, you simply haven't got them, and you can't buy them.

Yet we are supposed to be able to buy *anything—* and if we can't, we don't seem to know what to do. We don't seem to know where to go past that point. The illusion of being able to get inner happiness via outside sources eventually makes us crazy, makes us do completely crazy things. Even most psychotherapists are convinced that if a client doesn't pay a ridiculously hefty fee, he or she won't value the therapy. In a matter of about six seconds, if we are open to ourselves, we can spot this illusion dead center. In two more seconds we can see how we are victimized by it.

For example, which is crazier? The happy old man with his wood spirits or the following:

I go to buy a new car. I *know* that somehow, as soon as the last payment coupon is sent to the bank with a check, the car will begin to fall apart. I know that I can keep it alive only so long as I begin to pour countless dollars and cents into it: mufflers, starters, transmissions. First little bits and pieces begin to fail or fly away: wiper blades crumble; washers break off from door locks, and then finally the lock stems fall through the holes into the inaccessible door frames; the heater conks; adjustable seats flop back on broken hinges; seat belts spring loose from their moorings. It begins its death throes in its fourth cold winter.

I *know* this. It isn't hearsay. In most cases it's something we've experienced the frustration of, not just seen.

But I buy it. If, as may be the case, there is no alternative, then I am controlled. And I let myself be. I am now the prey of my materialistic upbringing which is coming back at me full force like a deadly boomerang.

Could it be that I *don't* know all of this? Maybe I only *think* I know. If I *really* knew, wouldn't I take proper action?

It isn't even an issue if I would rather see a gnome than get involved in a mess like this. The issue is that I have to see the truth of what is happening. But I won't do anything about it unless I see the truth of it first. Then *know* it.

If I buy that car willingly, knowing what I know, then I am buying it for status and self-esteem because I can't see them within myself. And so the car doesn't even belong to me: because I've bought it to impress somebody else. The car belongs to that somebody else. Nobody has anything—not really.

A tremendous split exists here between our inner "sense" and what we are supposed to "think" about the outside world.

EXPLORATION: It pays to see the *emotionally* illogical nature of what we are exposed to in our daily lives. One of the most startling ways to do this is to glance at the advertising spreads in any magazine—especially the cigarette ads.

Examine them from a single point of view: how they work nature into the display and sales pitch. There are all sorts of rugged men, pretty women, and beautiful couples, smoking cigarettes against backdrops of woods, waterfalls, streams. Sometimes there is a natural setting without a trace of people.

Be terribly critical: what's the powerful hidden meaning in such scenes?

The implication is strong that smoking is good for you. Not just unharmful, but *good*. Nature is good (that idea is still solid within us), so by association smoking is also good. Pure, natural, and beneficial.

Odd, but accurate. A completely "crazy" contradiction that we seem to accept with very little question.

We accept it because on some level we have come *not to see it.*

There is an important distinction to be made here. We don't accept this split by thinking, "Sure, smoking and nature go hand-in-hand." We accept it because the sense of our "inner seeing" has been short circuited; and so the bizarre contradiction, out there in the ad, has lost its ability to provide accurate feedback. The scene enters us almost subliminally, and provides some sort of justification when we next buy a pack of cigarettes—even though we know that they are destructive.

Keep picking up these contradictions: being aware of them keeps your critical judgment active and restores the feedback system that can help reconnect the inner life to the outer world. To *see* is to see clearly. Then action follows reflexively.

BEING CUT OFF

There is something about all this that many of us might not want to hear or face. By way of a hint, let me share with you one of my own past character traits. Many years ago I was driving with friends for an autumn weekend in the mountains. The scenery, I suppose, was beautiful, but I was busy hacking away at a crossword puzzle in the back seat. My friend's wife craned her head at me, then said in complete exasperation:

"Good grief! You're the only person I know who can drive through all of this with your head buried in a newspaper."

Red, orange, gold, umber: all that color was flowing past me as I looked up. And I was seeing none of it. I was too busy being involved in some intellectual competition with a bunch of little boxes, trying to find words for a "three-toed sloth" and a "Japanese paper screen."

I made some excuse about being tired; she clucked and turned back to the front. And as I continued to let the fall colors flow past me, I felt the beginnings of tears prickle my nose. A combination of self-pity—because I hadn't been able to get with the beauty of it all—and a deep, sad sense that I had cut myself off from something truly meaningful.

So it seems to me that one of the sure-fire ways we have of judging the lack of connection with our souls is confronting how sharply we may be cut off from what is natural in the world around us. All living things have "soul" —and if we are blind to it in the outside world, we are obviously blind to it in ourselves.

That is why the ecology-conservation movement has soul in it, because it recognizes that the smallest piece of nature has, ultimately, a profound meaning to human beings—both in terms of beauty as well as in terms of providing far-reaching life-support systems. Mind-boggling though it may be, the thinnest coating of moss on the trunk of a tree has something to do with the vegetables on our tables. And the sight of fall leaves, the ocean, a mountain, can lend us some peace, a moment of rest from the sickening pressures of our daily lives.

We might take a lesson from the Japanese, who work perhaps even harder than we do, but who seem to suffer much less from stress-related diseases. Rather than letting off a year's accumulation of pressure via a one-shot vacation, they make sure to rest, do nothing, for a little time each day. And during this rest they attempt to bring in a little of the natural world—a bud in a vase, some leaves on the floor.

Inside-outside.

To regain the connection, to let the energy and movement flow, we need to reestablish the mutual feedback system. And that is another aspect of the quiet, reflexive, potent work of the soul.

Now let's get deeply inside for a time. We have to look at thinking. Because thinking can be the prime vehicle for the kind of one-sided materialism we've been talking about. In fact thinking can actually *be* materialism.

4
The Thinking
Trap

Thinking is the most overrated activity of the human being. It has gotten overrated because the illusions of intellectual philosophy, perpetuated for hundreds of years, have taught us that thinking is what separates us from the beasts of the fields and jungles. Apparently we have needed that ego trip—the arrogance of the belief that we are so vastly superior to other living things.

And yet, lacking the capacity for "human thought," animals are rarely known to attack and kill their own kind. I have not heard of animals or plants waging wars. I have not heard of them turning against themselves or against nature—which is the same thing. I have never even heard of, or seen, a foolish animal, or an animal that doesn't know what to do—unless it has been incredibly brutalized or deprived of care from its earliest days.

We simply must ask ourselves a question that may be crucial for the continued existence of our entire planet:

With all our capacity for high-level thinking, how is it that we have brought ourselves closer and closer to global disaster? And how is it that, with all our massive brain power, we know so very little about ourselves?

I can't stress enough that we have misused thinking by making it a be-all and end-all, and applying it to areas where it does not belong. We have used it to create problems as well as to solve them—again because we use it in the wrong place. As a matter of fact, we generally end up using our brains in an effort to solve the very problems that they've created.

Thinking is the cause of most of our fears, rigidity, and sense of unreality about ourselves. The thoughts that flow in the process of thinking form the content of our unreality. Simply put, we think too much. We think too much, and thinking becomes unreality—but only if we use thinking where it doesn't belong. And we invariably do.

Just one example, in keeping with our theme, is that we may think that the soul does not exist because we can't see it. This is a useless thought because it has no place in the realm of the soul—which is based on feeling, sensing, intuition, inner "seeing," and knowing. It has as little place there as it does when you are making love, which for many people can be a profoundly emotional experience. Do we *see* an orgasm with our eyes? Can we even really describe it verbally? Sex therapists, for instance, can tell you that without a shadow of a doubt, thoughts interfere with lovemaking, whether they drift to the next day's work schedule, a movie just seen, the threat of a tax audit—or even to questions of performing well in the lovemaking itself. Which is why many therapists will try to get you to image or visualize a sexual scene—to at least get your thought process somewhere in line with what you are doing at the moment.

But this is extremely difficult because we are almost completely preoccupied with our thoughts, often of an unknowable future. At times they seem to be all that we have, seem to be us entirely—and so we miss what is going on at the moment. We lose the now in a swamp of thinking which in most cases is totally irrelevant to what we are doing or what our *being* is all about.

The person who tells you that "nothing is happening" is probably consumed by thoughts about the past and future. "Nothing is happening" always means that nothing is happening *now*. Notice the *is* in the comment; it means *now*, the present tense.

Also with many people who come to a therapist's office: nothing seems to be happening in their lives. Nothing *is*. There seems to be no *now*. Scratch the surface of that and you will find a bombardment of thoughts of the intensity of a cosmic shower; you almost have to duck.

EXPLORATION: See it for yourself. Watch what pops into your mind when you make love, when you are just relaxing, when you are talking to someone. See how you are really not tuned in to what you are engaged in at the moment. See how the thoughts are keeping you away from a full commitment to the present, the now. This is not a matter of intense concentration, of intense effort to keep tuned in; instead it is a matter of letting go of the thoughts.

This is why so many people give up meditation or the yoga class in which they enrolled so enthusiastically: they find themselves barraged by a clutter of thoughts that are painful and distracting—all of which produces another thought: I can't do this. So they give it up. Anyway, you see the chain reaction that is set off—like the people who worry about not sleeping.

THOUGHT AND ANXIETY

In the field of psychotherapy, most therapists I know use a relatively sound rule for knowing when they are anxious with a client even when they are not *feeling* anxious. The client says something and suddenly the therapist feels that he has to make a reply. The reply forms itself into words, and for several minutes, even for the entire session, the therapist keeps feeling that he *has* to say this sentence— even when the client has left his original statement far behind in time. And of course the therapist's comment would no longer make any sort of sense.

It is the need to put this thought into words, the having to, that clues the therapist into the idea that he is anxious—that he has not been listening to his client but only to something personal that wants to pop out of himself. In other words he is listening to himself instead of to the client. And there are times when the therapist doesn't know this at all—as when he is trying to place the "material" of his client into a theoretical framework, into a set of ideas. Again, he is listening only to himself: because it is *his* theory, not the client's.

We all do this in our daily encounters with others. And we do it incessantly.

Thoughts, used in the wrong places, may not only provoke anxiety, they may *be* the anxiety itself, but deadened out of feeling. I dare not feel, so I think. I dare not feel an attack, so I begin to frame an argument in thoughts. So that the thinking doesn't just mask the anxiety, it *becomes* the anxiety. Any time thinking is used in a nonintellectual context, it *is* anxiety.

So when, for example, you "can't" listen to someone at a social gathering, but begin to think of your response before the person is finished speaking—then you are anxious, you are out of touch with the flow, with what you feel, and a connection with yourself and the other is impossible.

A client of mine, a literature scholar of great talent, nevertheless could not admit to not having read any book that was brought up in conversation. He would say that he had read the book, then keep attuned to any device through which he could avoid revealing that he really hadn't read it. Which obviously made him terribly uncomfortable and led to his ending many encounters quickly; he would simply escape the situation. This pattern finally gave him so much anxiety that he decided never to lie again. And when he eventually admitted to a woman that he hadn't read a particular book, he described it this way:

"When I said I hadn't read it, I felt as if some kind of abyss opened up and I was about to fall into it. For a moment I was blown away; I could feel myself shake; I wanted to get out of that room as fast as I could—in fact I remember looking around for the door. And then she said: 'Well, you have a real treat in store for you when you do read it. I almost wish I hadn't so I could get the original feeling back again.'"

Now how about this: my client and this woman became lovers, and as far as I can tell they've been happy for a couple of years in a relationship of real meaning. And he learned a few other things: that books were not just work. They could be treats; they had real feeling in them.

And if he had not stopped lying he probably would

not even have remembered the woman's name or what she looked like.

Thinking not only creates anxiety, but the anxiety in thinking keeps us away from ourselves and from each other. In my client's case—and you have probably figured this out—he had terribly low self-esteem despite his outward success and his brilliant mind.

But low self-esteem doesn't *exist*.

You have to *think* you have low self-esteem. And we'll see how this works in a following chapter.

So because my client thought he had low self-esteem he had to devise a whole thought-pattern, an intricate web of defensive thoughts, to keep away from the anxiety based solely on the thought that he had low self-esteem. A bottomless ocean of thoughts.

It's not complicated at all. See it in yourself. I am not talking about anything even remotely connected with the Power of Positive Thinking. Positive thinking can be just as time consuming and wasteful as anything else because ultimately it doesn't work by clicking a switch or turning gears. You can't reverse negativism overnight by memorizing a list of platitudes.

Just see what you do with your thoughts. See what purpose they serve when you're using them outside of where they belong—outside the area of the pure intellect, such as reading a book steeped in philosophical ideas or mathematical concepts, or solving logical problems whose solutions *require* logic—in short in any area where it is obvious that $2 \times 2 = 4$. Or $E = mc^2$.

Again, therapists, when they try to fit a client into a theory of personality, are desperately searching for a $2 \times 2 = 4$. And many will get it to turn out that way—

even if the end formula has very little to do with the client. The magic word here is "because." My client does this *because* he was beaten by his father; he is angry not at me, but at the bad father I represent, etc.

But the vast, vast majority of people don't act or feel like the simple equation. They don't even act like $E = mc^2$ —a more complicated but still predictable equation (though their anger when you push theory at them may well assume atom-bomb proportions). People are, despite their traps, ultimately free.

Remember: to develop our possibilities we must get "round the rules" of science as we have always known them. Which, to stress the point again, means to see things in new ways.

Thinking, for example, not only gives rise to an inability to see things clearly, it is the cause of most of our fears, stiffness, and sense of personal unreality. The thoughts that emerge in the process of thinking form the content of unreality. But again, this is true only where thinking doesn't belong.

Thinking does not belong anywhere where 2×2 may not $= 4$. This is the realm of feeling, intuition, soul stuff— the gut feeling (not a blind compulsive impulse) that tells you something of great importance. And this is what interests us here. It is also the world of dreams and inner visions where 2×2 almost *never* $= 4$. We all know that dreams produce incredible combinations of images that lead to something quite unexpected—and it has been this refusal of dreams to bend to waking logic that has resulted in expressions such as "It's only a dream." We tend to dismiss what we can't wedge into our five senses even if it applies to ourselves, even if it is our own production.

Too often we take this world of intuition and feeling,

cut its heart out, and turn our backs. But it keeps plaguing us; it continues trying to tell us something despite our selves.

Our dreams are *us*, ourselves, trying to inform ourselves, but too often we don't listen—even though the reality of the dream can be more vivid than the reality of waking life. And that's when we become terribly lost; because we dismiss ourselves as our best source of knowledge and experience. And yet only *we* can truly inform ourselves.

We do this not only with dreams. We show it by our attitudes and value judgments and belief systems. We are always mouthing the words and thoughts of others so reflexively that we think they are ours. They come to *seem* like ours.

Let me illustrate: I have an eleven-year-old cousin, a bright, feeling, sensitive girl, a star pupil in her private school. One day we got into the topic of teachers—good ones, bad ones, indifferent ones—and I asked her what she thought made a good one. She said that a teacher should be intelligent, exciting, interesting, should like children, and be nice—"but not too nice." When I asked what "too nice" meant, she said:

"Well, if a teacher is too nice you take advantage of her."

From what I know of my cousin, it was hard to believe that she could take advantage of anyone, and I snapped:

"Come on, Lucy! When have you ever taken advantage of a nice teacher?"

In a moment it was clear that she never had. She had simply mouthed something that she had heard, without once questioning it—and yet it was completely foreign to her own knowledge and experience. And she was accepting it. This is terribly important: *she had no personal experience of an attitude that she put forth as her own belief.*

This may seem a small story, a trivial anecdote—a small child, a small situation, small consequences. But reflect for a minute: here is a child who already at the age of eleven has learned not to trust her own knowledge and *perceptions,* but to accept the thoughts, the rules, the "shoulds" and "of courses" of others. Without question, like the reflex of a primitive organism. And thinks they are hers. And it is not—at least not yet—that she feels all her personal experiences are contradicted; it is that she is coming to believe reflexively that her experiences are somehow of no use—*as if they are missing.* And who knows how deeply this gap may deepen into other areas of her life: sex, marriage, career, and all the rest of the ingredients of adult life.

Thoughts have begun to overwhelm, to transplant, her knowledge and experience.

And note the content: the thought has made her suspicious of people who are "too nice." Mightn't that simply become people who are just "nice?" After all, "too" is a relative term. And if we begin to suspect what could be good contact with another we lose the connection, our soul begins to erode at the edges.

FEELING EMPTY

This is one of the powerful reasons why we say we feel empty, unconnected. Yet no one is empty. But you can feel empty if your own experience is crushed by empty thoughts—especially when they have the authority of "have to's."

I had a client, a very deep woman capable of feeling an enormous amount of beauty. She could never say "I want," only "I have to." Her whole orientation to other people hinged on such statements: "I *have* to go shopping for clothes"; "I *have* to go to an opera to get information for a course paper"; "I *have* to stay home Saturday night because my mother is sick." The list was endless. But in nine out of ten cases she was doing what she wanted— and knew it. It was just that she seemed afraid to use the magic word—*want*. She was aware that because she had painted herself to others as a person who had so many obligations, she was—in her thinking—seen as a very responsible person. For complex reasons of little importance here, this was an image she needed desperately to project to the world. A thoroughly responsible, mature, unselfish, perhaps even martyrish person.

"And yet," I said to her, "you're extremely irresponsible."

When she got done being angry, she asked me what I had meant. I told her.

"Because if you let everybody know that you *want* to do all these things, you'd have to take responsibility for everything you do because it would be your choice. No *want* is no choice, no responsibility."

She assumed that no one would question the authority of the "have to," just as Cousin Lucy absorbed the authority of the statement about the teacher.

EXPLORATION: Hunt down an area in yourself similar to Lucy's or to my client's. Find something you "believe in"—not something you know or have experienced or have seen. You don't have to start big—like your religion or your atheism. Start with something you accept without questioning if it is true—something about a person you know, a belief system held by someone else, even a statement such as "The Presidency is an office to which small men rise and become great," "Responsible people should vote even if neither candidate has merit." You will find something if you bead in on it—but remember that it's hard to do because we are not very aware—as with Lucy— that the things in which we "believe" may not be part of our own experience.

Whatever you find, you will then see that you have been accepting only a *thought*—and often a thought that never originated with you. And certainly not from your own experience. Somebody has *told* you this—whether a parent, a friend, or a whole society.

Let's see how this thinking trap works on two levels —one a bit removed, the other very familiar. Some years ago in Europe there convened a large interfaith conference of Eastern and Western spiritual disciplines and religions. Those delegates—whether Christian monks, Jewish mystics, or Eastern gurus—who meditated regularly and over time were able to make contact directly with inner experiences they shared; all got along well, mingled souls. But all at the conference was not peace and brotherhood.

There was intense quarreling, debate, and anger—but only among those people who were involved in the intellectual and nonexperiential aspects of their faiths. They quibbled over points of dogma, over what is truth—over, of course ultimately, who is right.

It was inevitable. It is always inevitable when thinking substitutes for knowing.

Now for a stark, but tricky, example, a concern of millions: the "pain" of childbirth. Women who have never given birth can only "learn" of the "pain" from mothers. They cannot learn it themselves, but they—the vast majority—accept it as fact. But they can't say: I *know* that the pain *is*. So for them it can only be a thought, a thought with powerful social clout behind it.

It's a thought that begins to arouse fear from the moment of pregnancy, and keeps it aroused straight into the delivery room—and by that time the body and mind are so woven into the web that the absence of pain becomes *impossible*. The thought has created the fear.

Bearing on this, I actually overheard the following at at party:

> First Woman: How was your delivery?
> Second Woman: It was a beautiful experience for me.
> First Woman: I'm not looking forward to it.
> Second Woman: The first isn't always *that* rough.
> First Woman: I could live without it. I want to be out cold.

There are a minority of women in our society who, without drugs or some variant of natural childbirth techniques, *don't* experience the pain. There are whole "primitive" cultures whose women don't feel this pain at all: *because the thought of the pain simply does not exist in that particular culture.*

Yet another thought: a number of psychiatrists and psychologists will tell you that *not* feeling this pain is a sign of some kind of neurosis or worse. It doesn't seem to matter that many of these experts are men or childless women.

And in our society children can be absolutely terrified of a visit to the dentist without ever having been in the chair—and even in the company of their parents. There is no gene labelled *Dentist-Fear*. Somewhere . . . somewhere . . . they have a thought.

More focus on the problem: we are always thinking instead of being or just plain living—and this thinking is always an illusion when it is used where it doesn't belong. But we don't even have a sense of the illusion except when it is too late and we find ourselves completely fragmented, in pieces, with only an idea of what we've done, how we've behaved, but not who we are.

And the thought-illusion is used not only in an effort to bring "happiness" but, as above, to stimulate our fears.

For instance, if I earn a great deal of money, buy a huge showplace house, and dress like the models in the *New York Times* men's fashions section, that is somehow going to bring more happiness. How? I can't *know* that it will—but I believe it will because I am told so by the advertisers and the culture. I might be admired, respected, or bitterly envied. But how am I happy? All I am is standing there being looked at, reacted to, and not even as me, but only as what I look like.

If we ever really feel better about ourselves because we wear new clothes, then we know we're in trouble.

As my client who suffered the massive heart attack said: "I always wanted a great big car to drive down the streets of all those people who said I couldn't make it. To zonk them. But then where would *I* be? If I used the car that way it wouldn't be mine, it wouldn't belong to me. The whole display would be for *them*."

This very modern insight with its very modern symbol is not so far removed from the Buddha realizing the foolishness of his early asceticism because all it really meant was that he was just as tied to the material world as if he

were a hedonist—because it was so important that everyone could see him giving up his possessions.

This is also what I meant when I said that thoughts
can be materialistic—because what we call "reality" is always concrete, always that which you can see, touch, have
proven to you. In short, reality becomes materialism. And
so can the thoughts, because we will have a thought about
the future which hasn't arrived yet—the pain of childbirth,
for example, the retaliation of my boss if I ask for a raise,
etc.—*and then we treat this illusory, fantasied thought as if
it were real, as if it is truth.* And then act on it, or not act
on it.

So we will perform some real action or behavior based
on the illusion. On pure ether.

IF . . . THEN

This sequence should be familiar to all of us: "What if"
or "If I do this, then. . . ." If I become angry at my father,
he will disown me. If I ask for a raise I will be fired. If I
have to give a speech I'll get anxious. If I believe in the
soul people will think I'm crazy. If I don't go to church I
will be sent to hell. If I let go and live my own life I
won't have any friends left.

Unhappily, the list is endless.

And yet it is all an incredible illusion—but it can
serve, like my client's "have to" and "shoulds," to avoid
truly taking responsibility for oneself.

We can't know what will happen; we can't predict
the future—yet we use what isn't there to stop being ourselves, to block off and dam up our internal energy and
wisdom. To imprison the soul.

It's worth underlining that we accept these illusions,

these fictions, as realities. Not as possibilities—possibilities are always fresh, new, expansive, exciting, ways to growth —but as realities. I am *sure* I'll be fired if I ask for a raise. I am *sure*. Yet I cannot *possibly* know.

So in treating these thoughts as realities, we can easily come to base our lives on them. And this turns not only our thoughts, but also our lives, into illusions. And *there* is the sense of emptiness, of unreality, of the loss of soul.

Let's suppose that little Lucy fails to trust her experience and keeps her illusion of the "too nice" teacher as a "reality"—as a person who is (actually *has to be*) taken advantage of. Here are only a few of the dismal potentialities:

She can begin to bait the "too-nice" teachers because that is what one is supposed to do, and besides, it's hip to humiliate adults; or she can self-righteously *not* try to take advantage of them, thereby placing herself via fantasy in a superior position to the other children in her class.

Some day she might want to be a teacher herself, but cannot because she might think of herself as a too-nice person and not want to be manipulated by the children or young adults; or she might become a teacher and strike the fragmented, unreal pose of a disciplinarian or iceberg so as not to be taken advantage of.

Or—painful but hardly improbable—she may become a teacher and the original thought might be so important to preserve—because she may desperately have to be right about it—that she may become a teacher and be artificially "nice" *in order* to have the children take advantage of her. By that time of life she may have to be right instead of knowing what is true. You could call that kind of life one of moral masochism.

None of this is impossible because it happens every day a million times over.

All of this is a series of sequences based on one thought. But even a small pocket of illusion can lead to a disconnected soulless life.

Of course the truth is *what is,* not what one *thinks.* The expression *really* is, "I am therefore I think." The other way around is a way of playing a stupid and dangerous, though very intellectual, game with human existence. I hardly have to tell you that whole systems of religions, philosophies, and psychotherapies have been based, and continue to be based, on *thoughts* about people, not on what people are themselves about. And so have whole lives.

But see how the parts are related to the whole:

Individual: A brilliant, esteemed, highly intellectual, well-known professional Catholic man disinherits his only son, refuses to have any contact with him, because he marries a Jewish woman. I have personally experienced this man; I left his presence feeling chilled.

Social: In India, in 1948, on the eve of the division of the subcontinent into India and Pakistan, there was a bloodbath between Muslim and Hindu the likes of which the modern world may never see again short of a nuclear catastrophe.

What the man has done has led to what the groups of people have done. If you want to bring the package into the same area, then make the Catholic man a Hindu who disinherited his son because the youth took up with a Muslim girl.

The human connection is broken because of what looks like an idea, a thought—because someone will not experience the unity of the soul that keeps us all together.

An idea, an illusion, has been converted into the reality of a broken relationship, a holocaust of violence.

And if I have the thought that I don't have to become aware of my own anger, my own dark hidden rage, then I might as well have my finger on the red button that might explode the world into particles of hydrogen.

We have to emerge from this if we are to regain the full meaning and power of our souls.

And it must start individually, with each of us. Social action won't do it for us.

OUT OF THE TRAP

A happier note: one of my clients entered therapy with me after a brief stay in a west-coast clinic after he tried to commit suicide by an overdose of sleeping pills. I was warned by his former therapist—and rightly so—that this man had many suicidal *thoughts*. One of which he had obviously acted upon. Suicidal thinking is taken very seriously by psychotherapists, but often they treat these thoughts as if they were real and not thoughts to be gotten into, explored, and followed. The rule of thumb seems to be to seal them over, stop them by drugs if possible, and never follow them. Instead, they try to find some way in which the person can derive more enjoyment from the "realities" of the environment—which is of course exactly what such a person is trying to tell you he wants no part of—the environment itself. But if you are a therapist who sees himself as deriving meaning and "pleasure" *only* from the environment, where else can you help a client get to?

In the vast majority of cases this approach is a total failure—and the likelihood of failure is supercharged by the therapist's fright of a possible suicide in his practice—a

fright that ranges from a deep sense of having failed another human being to the more superficial reason that
the therapist will be criticized by his colleagues.

We did something very different, this client and I. He
didn't want to be sealed over and he didn't want to take
stop-gap medication and he didn't want to hear supportive
statements about the potential pleasures of life in Newark,
New Jersey. He wanted to get rid of his thoughts, and
he didn't care where the chips fell.

I did, but I followed his lead, took courage from his
stand, and went with him.

He had many dreams and thoughts about plunging
out a window. In the dreams he would wake before he
hit the ground, screaming and in total panic; and he
would stop his thoughts as soon as he was perched on a
windowsill or the railing of a high balcony.

We didn't seal up.

We used his fantasies, dreams, and images to get him
up on the windowsill—and out.

With his eyes closed, sitting in a state of relaxation,
and with me, I suppose, as his support, he imagined himself at his desk in his living room. He began to look
at the window and began to feel—not think—the panic of
the window, the height, the distance down. For a brief
moment he tried to stay rooted in his chair at the desk,
to drive the thought away—but then he let himself get up
and walk toward the window, and mumbled almost inaudi-
bly, "Are you here, Paul?"

"Yes."

In the vibrant inner world, with his eyes closed sitting
in my office, he walked to the window and slowly opened it,
almost moaning:

"Oh, my God, I'm going to be mangled, there's going

to be blood and bits and pieces all over—and God, the pain. . . ."

And then, through the window inside him, he leaped. And began to fall, let himself fall.

He never hit bottom.

Half way down he began to fly.

It must always have been a possibility.

And there was no more need for the thoughts.

5
Getting Beneath the Thoughts

My client, of course, visualized his jump through the window. Not fantasized. *Visualized*. This is a crucial difference, and I will devote a whole section to this difference later.

He let the power of his inner life take charge—and by doing so, he saw the true meaning of his all-consuming obsession and fear in the outer world.

Now we would all agree that suicide is a very dramatic event, preceded by what are obviously very dramatic thoughts. Not everyone has suicidal thoughts—but many of us do, without revealing them, without being open about them. On the other hand, we have all had thoughts that, in our own lives, in the space within which we move, are no less meaningful, important, or upsetting. And as with suicidal thoughts, our goal is very often to avoid them, try to put them out of our heads, perhaps even drink or smoke them away. Our tendency is not to go *through* them, not to examine them, not to see why they exist.

That way we seem to get some temporary rest from them, from their pain or annoyance, but they remain just beneath the surface of our awareness. Although *we* hold on to *them*, the experience of it is that they have us in their grip: they flood us as if from outside.

What is it about thoughts that make them so powerful, make them seem like forces that attack us or eat us up from the outside—almost as if they don't exist within us? This is an important question, because our tendency is to hope that we can get rid of our problems via some outside device. Thus, without meaning to, we lure ourselves away from the inside, away from the soul, and rely on outside "cures." So that we find ourselves in the wrong place.

This is again what I mean when I stress that thoughts can be, and often are, a form of materialism. Seen as outside forces, they seem so *real*.

As with the "suicidal" person who keeps trying to tell us (in his misbalanced way) that he finds nothing of value in the external world, and we keep trying to tell him (in *our* misbalanced way) that there is everything of value out there, so too with all the tortuous thoughts that plague us. We jump from one pole to another. Instead of looking at the thoughts and seeing if they make any sense, we try to leap away somewhere to get rid of them.

For example, say I feel lonely and my thought is that this is a bad place to be in, that loneliness (which we often confuse with being alone) is awful, that it means I am cut off, or that I must be a terrible person, or that other people are horrible, or that to stop my loneliness I should go to bed with somebody or get married. Whatever.

Because a powerful thought in our society is that pain or emotional suffering is bad and shouldn't be, I'm apt to *do* something about this "loneliness." I may go to a singles bar to stop my "pain," but the chances are that I will walk into a situation of true loneliness—as one of my clients tersely put it, into a "flesh market" where chances of real contact are all but impossible. And then I despair.

What is it that I haven't done between the thoughts and the frustrating action? What I haven't done is look into my loneliness and see that it is a condition inside of myself, not a condition outside. *I* am lonely, inside. *I* am detached, disconnected from something life-giving within myself. I am alienated from *me*—and so I feel alienated from out there.

It should seem obvious, even if we use the logical formula of the $2 \times 2 = 4$, that if there is a problem within, that's where we should go. Except that we are trained to look away from ourselves, and with this kind of training, inside is the last place we think of looking.

FACING OUR DEPENDENCY

What we are, then, is dependent. Very dependent. On the outside—as we were on our parents. And this is a point that needs to be repeated over and over until it is absorbed, until we can see it as a major component of the human condition instead of as a source of shame. What is, *is*. To eradicate it we must first *see* it.

We can cut it any way we wish, but when we cut it straight down to the bone, what keeps us in prison, away from the energy of our souls, is a tremendous unquestioned dependency on the outside world. This is something we don't like to look at because we don't want to feel weak, small. But that is what our almost crazed pursuit of security seems to be all about. Our thoughts, and the fear they arouse, become part and parcel of our security systems and we find it hard to give up the package. *We become our security needs instead of becoming ourselves.* And security always represents a past position that gets projected onto the future. A need for security is never a *now* position.

Let's see how this can work and create a deadly downward spiral.

I know a man whose goal in life has always been security. In considering a career while in college, his security needs led him to be completely "practical." While he had lots of interests and could get excited by lots of intellectual things, he decided to become a high-school teacher. Of course there is nothing wrong about becoming a high-school teacher, but the reason for his decision was based not on a going-toward-something, but on a careful appraisal of past history. He saw (we are talking about the early 1950's) that based on the past, all one had to do was graduate college with a degree in education in order to get an instant job with all the fringe benefits of health insurance, pension, tax-deductible travel, purchasing plans, etc. In sum, in the 1950's you couldn't lose your job once you were secure in the public-school system.

The main illusion here is the idea that *nothing changes.* That what was in the past, is now, and ever shall be. And the trend of the personality that developed from the acceptance of this illusion was a commitment to personal stagnation.

Over the course of years, he widened the circle of security to include a wife who began to teach in the same system; then he began to teach in summer school and lead extracurricular activities for additional income. With all this sense of security, he felt he could buy a house, which he did, and a car.

And then the crash came as budgets were slashed in the mid-1960's. Suddenly younger teachers were being excessed; summer-school teaching was cut; there was no more money available for extracurricular supervision; insurance benefits were watered down.

The man's wife is no longer working and finds it all but impossible to get a job in a private school because of her now socially redundant teaching specialty. She has to find another specialty—but literally is not interested in another one. Their house is partially supported by her father who fortunately has some extra money. And the man has had to drop out of his doctoral program to find a part-time job.

We have to realize that there is no such thing as outside security unless we remain infants. Or we can never see life as it is, but only as we want it or need it to be.

Outside security simply does not exist.

If we believe that it does, and we try to cling to it, any sort of change becomes destructive to us, must frighten us, because change then has to represent a threat to our entire position.

In order to maintain our illusory security it is vital that nothing change. One change topples the whole system, because the system is based on a concept of ourselves as immobile, rigid, and static. And if that is the position in which we place ourselves, we *must* be swept up each time a change occurs in the outside world. Literally swept up— and dashed down—like the high-school teacher. And here is the paradox that eludes us all the time: that if we immobilize ourselves like pinned butterflies while forces move around us, we have no power at all. So that anything at all can push us around. We have clutched to the past and have turned ourselves into that piece of glass that the mechanical hammer will always break. Remember the biblical story of Lot's wife who became a pillar of salt because she looked back—*looked backward?*

When we seek external security we are giving up control—and yet control is the very thing we hoped to get from the security.

EXPLORATION: See how the need for security has worked in your life. See that whatever you own, whomever you rely upon, is part of that security system. Look at your job: you work for someone or some organization, and you can be cut loose with a snap of the fingers. Your spouse can leave you. Your mortgage can be foreclosed. At any minute the rug can be entirely pulled out from under your material existence. *Feel the threat and anxiety in this.* Now carefully explore all the aspects of your life that you have chosen due to security needs. See what you have given up to protect you against disaster. And be aware that there is no protection at all. Emotional protection is not covered by an insurance policy. Since there really is no security, can you try to sense your way into some alternatives, some different ways you might want to live? And if you simply examine your security traps, you can see how dependent you have become on them, how you have come to fear their removal.

We have no control at all when we give away our power to a person or a thing. And when we give away the power we come to fear what we have given it to, then come to be angry at it or hate it, because we think it has power over us—without the realization that we have given over *our* power *to* it.

Nothing has power over us unless we give it permission.

My client has a dream. He goes to a store with his

mother to buy a suit. He picks one he likes and waits for his mother to pay for it. She says she has no money. There is a moment of panic. Then he remembers his wallet, looks into it, and discovers that he has enough money to pay for the suit.

Significantly, right at that point he switches from the dream and asks me how long his therapy will take. I tell him:

"When you don't have to 'remember' that you have your wallet."

That's how we give up our inner power. We look to others to do for us while all the time we can do perfectly well for ourselves.

Security is like alcohol. The more you drink the more you get filled, yet the more you want. And then you lose consciousness.

The fear of losing the security causes us to hang on, to clutch, to grasp. In a perverse way our old thoughts are security just because they *are* old, because they come from a past system—and the past is always security because the past is what we know. What has happened to us in the past, what we have thought about in the past, is like a powerful magnet sucking us back from movement.

That's why we hang on to suffering as well. Because it's something we seem to be used to. Who among us hasn't asked: Why do I *do* this? Why do I torture myself this way? Am I a masochist? How *can* I be? I don't get any pleasure out of pain.

It's not a question of pleasure out of pain. It's a question of security. Security in the ossified thought-patterns.

Here's a tortuous pattern of thoughts that many men will find painfully familiar:

We fall in love with a woman, we make love to her

and she responds warmly and openly. Being open, one day she tells us that she has had lovers in the past. This may be no great revelation, and "intellectually" we want to pay little attention to the fact; we are aware of certain freedoms in our modern age.

But we really can't accept it at all: we have incessant thoughts and fantasies about the past lovers, and they may grow and expand until in a burst of anger and abuse we may smash the relationship.

We can't see that the women have chosen *us*. We can only think that we have been betrayed—*in the past*.

On the other side of the coin, women who marry divorced men frequently can't accept the *fact* of the new marriage. They resent, even hate, the former wife—as if she is still important, a perpetual living threat.

Here there is no real acceptance of the present living situation, only a clinging to a past pattern. And a feeling of utter powerlessness—all based on thoughts that seem like realities.

We just can't seem to give up what has gone before. New territory, experimentation, seem incredible risks. But only by risk, by taking chances, do we take control and power back into our own hands.

We must look at the old habits, see them and feel them—or nothing will change; we can't think our way out of them. And the trouble is that we rarely *experience* our habits; we just carry them out reflexively, like second nature. But we *can* experience them if we slow down, if we let ourselves.

Take smoking. No matter where we are, we light up, puff away, then toss the butt some place. Almost never do we sit still, light the thing, and focus intently, with all our concentration, on the act itself. Which means that we are having no experience of it. Now we may have nagging, anxious thoughts that we should quit smoking because it is dangerous and may eventually kill us. But the difficulty in giving up smoking lies partly in the fact that we don't really know what we're doing, what we are really giving up. *And we can't give up something that we haven't experienced.*

So that we have no consciousness of it—only a reflexive habit (and how many times have smokers lit up only to find that when they perch the cigarette in the ashtray another one is already there?) and maybe the thought that we should give it up because medical science has shown its harmful effects. But thinking can't make us give it up. Anyone who has tried will see this as a painful truth.

But we can accomplish a great deal by focusing awareness.

FOCUSING ON THOUGHTS

And we can focus on thoughts themselves.

EXPLORATION: Sit quietly with your eyes closed, with no purpose or goal at all, and just be aware of the incredible amount of thoughts that suddenly start to barrage you. You needn't worry—because worry will just be a thought about the thoughts. Watch them flood in and become aware of how they prevent a sense simply that you are sitting quietly. See how we all put this clutter and noise in the way of our peace and quietness. And then we can see how, and why, we feel that we can so seldom relax—and how thinking can constantly wear us out as if we have done ten straight hours of backbreaking physical work. In this Exploration, it's not the content of the thoughts that matter—it's sheerly the *amount* of them.

As I mentioned before, we are aware of this flood often before sleep—but then what we focus on is the trouble with sleeping. Let's try to be aware in a fully conscious situation, a situation without anxiety built into it.

To rediscover the power within ourselves, to get back the connection with our souls, our energy, we *must* sit quietly and experience ourselves—not get perpetually lost in what we *do*. You could call this meditation, but the word isn't necessary, and the process isn't fancy or complicated.

A natural question arises now, which is likely to be: Sitting quietly is all well and good, but what do I *do* about it? How can I *get rid* of the thoughts? How can I drive them out?

The answer is that you can't *do anything* about them. Nor can you get rid of them nor drive them away. The doing, getting rid of, driving away, are all words that we are used to in our emphasis on activity, on action—sometimes just for the sake of it. That's like the example of loneliness and the singles bar—a jump to action without seeing what goes on between the thought and the action. And the result would be identical: frustration. Doing, action, are outside words, not inside words; and when you are going inside, action is irrelevant.

We have to learn to be receptive to the inside, not to be active—and this is very difficult because we are brought up to be active and to believe that the opposite of activity is passivity—and that is a "bad" word. Except that passivity is not the issue. Passivity is accepting a position in life from which you won't, or feel you "can't," move. It is *receptivity* that we are interested in now—and the opening of ourselves to ourselves.

So we can't *do* anything about the thoughts because

that would be turning them into even more materiality—because we can only do something to something concrete. We can only watch our thoughts, see them—and perhaps for the first time in our lives actually know, actually experience, that they are there, everywhere, often useless, nonsensical, and blocks to our energy.

It is an incredible realization to see how we won't let our thoughts leave us alone.

To relocate our souls we have to be quiet with ourselves and give up the security of our thoughts—but we can't even begin to see that they give us security until we recognize how we pester ourselves with them. We seem always to need to keep them with us. And to let go of them as best we can means to release a vast amount of bottled up, wasted energy—the energy poured into keeping them alive. The energy needs to be freed and to be put back into the process of living. We need to take a chance, to get thinking out of our emotional lives, and put it out where it belongs—in the area of nonemotional problem-solving and intellectual activity.

Only a person who existed totally in the realm of the head could ever have coined the phrase, *I think therefore I am*. Look at the phrase closely and you can see the madness lurking beneath its clever philosophical glitter.

But security *is* what we *think* we know (like the teacher who thought that his profession would keep him safe and protected forever)—but rarely, if ever, what we *truly* know. Remember how my cousin Lucy might root a major part of her life in a thought—and one she hadn't even produced herself?

When we get into a position of what we *think* is security, the thoughts begin to spin off it like spokes in a turning wheel. I buy a house in a suburb and, although I have always considered myself a liberal and all that that means, I suddenly find myself panicked when I hear that a black family might move in down the street. So I *thought* I was a liberal; but suddenly I am not, as a result of another thought that creeps in: property values will plummet because a black has moved into the neighborhood. Where am *I* in all of this? Who *am* I? Do *I* discover down deep that *I* am really a bigot? Maybe, maybe not. But I certainly can realize that I haven't looked at what I've been thinking of myself for years.

EXPERIENCING

There is no getting around it. We are not going to feel, sense, anything unless we experience it. Otherwise it all stays in the world of ideas and thoughts—in the head, somebody else's truth or even somebody else's lie. It doesn't matter. What matters is that it's not our experience. And if it isn't our experience it's meaningless, it may not even exist except in the ether.

That's why I can't pep-talk you or myself—I can only suggest that you get quiet with yourself when you are looking inside, or be very critical and clear about the things you see on the outside. I can't tell you that you and I are terrific—and stop there because that's what we want to hear for the glory of our egos—or give you or myself some list of rules to follow on the path to *nirvana*.

We each have to experience ourselves in our own ways—*but we have to experience* if we are to get to the bottom of ourselves. And I think that this great need to experience is reflected in so many of the "movements" we see all around us these days—Transcendental Meditation, est, variations of "self-control," and a host of others.

Some universal, underlying realization exists that we have been accepting a whole lot of so-called truths without ever once feeling them to be true to ourselves.

We often immerse ourselves in "movements" and often packaged "ways" to "consciousness-expansion" because we can be so thoroughly and naively American, in the sense that we have all become habitual victims of consumerism and the out-there way of life. If there are pills for our pain, and TV games for our boredom, and all sorts of external remedies for everything—then why, damn it, isn't there some similar technological way to get in touch with ourselves?

Because there just isn't.

Only *we* can do it—by ourselves. We can flit from "movement" to "movement," use "technique" after "technique"—only to drop out of them. We are too impatient—and it is this very impatience that causes us to grasp at any "way" or method that promises a quick answer.

There are no quick ways; in fact, speed itself has brought us to the point where we are bowing under our burdens and want, *need* to, slow down before we collapse.

There is only *our* way—and to find *our* way is to find *our* soul. And that requires patience and discovering our own pace. So we might as well toss out all the rules and regulations of the movements. Then relax, see ourselves, and get into our own flow without worrying about goals, time limits, and keeping pace with some invisible competitor.

And the point remains: that if we do not focus on *ourselves*, become aware of *our* habits, reflexive ideas, and the thoughts that aren't even us but have gotten inside us —then we will never take a chance and break out of the cocoon, the womb, of our security—but a security that has as much substance as thin air. It can hurt to get out, and we are not going to soft-pedal that.

It seems to be like this:

My client is focusing on a "lump" in his throat, a lump that has been stuck there for over thirty years. To him, it has always felt like a real, solid thing, and it has taken him a very long time to realize that it is in some way connected to his asthma. Some sort of invisible obstruction in his breathing apparatus.

He begins to visualize the lump and sees it as a piece of fleshy matter, then attempts to work with it, to see if he can alter its size, control it without effort. After a time he is very successful at this: he can make it small, very small, until he is no longer able to feel it. Suddenly he senses that his throat and chest expand, open, become what he calls "a vast space."

But then he begins to see the lump growing again and without struggling he lets it, just lets it take over. It swells until it completely surrounds him like a huge egg. Inside, he feels himself pleasantly immersed in water, warm water, and lets himself move and float slightly—and is aware that *he does not want to get out*. It is not frightening at all. He says, "It's nice in here"—and senses a bit later that he can't really *do* anything. His hands don't work properly; like a tiny infant he has no grasp reflex. But he is comfortable, peaceful, untroubled.

Only by a slow process can he finally leave the place, and only after much pain.

What happened here was that the asthma, the lump in the throat, was experienced by him all his life as a pain, a torture, tremendous anxiety in his inability to breathe, fears of strangling, death. But he was totally unaware that underneath it all the lump really cocooned him like a warm, water-filled womb from which he didn't want to emerge. So in clinging to his suffering he was really clinging to his womb-like "security," but without any awareness of this whatever. And therefore any thought that spun off his asthma, the lump, such as, "I am afraid I am dying," "I am strangling to death," "I can't find my spray," "I will never make it to the doctor"—all these painful, terrifying thoughts really represented his "security." But it represented the security of what lay beneath the pain: the security of that womb, the sense of which, until his visualization, he hadn't the faintest conscious clue.

I can't say it any better than his visualization showed it. He just had to experience the false security, know that the womb existed within him and understand that it trapped his life—that *he* was trapping his life—before he could get up the courage to leave it.

And his outer life, his life of behavior, his life with himself and with others, had for years been completely dominated by his symptoms. He couldn't exercise or play sports, which he loved; he was afraid of becoming too excited on dates for fear of an asthma attack; he avoided any place where a cat might be; and on and on—thought after thought—everything that seemed like pain, all in the service of keeping him in that womb.

The womb, the need for security, kept him disconnected from himself, from taking risks, from looking inside.

But finally he did it and a whole life began to change.

This is the kind of thing we will find when we begin to look at ourselves: we will find our wombs, the way we have constructed them, the way they keep us trapped, and that beneath all our feelings of pain, frustration, and often hopelessness, there is a powerful sense of not wanting to get out. That we keep our own pain and troubles going because we don't want to get out, because we don't even know we're in there.

And finally we can cut the cord.

6
The Illusion
of Choice

How important is choice? Making choices? Is freedom, is connection with the energy of the soul, a result of our capacity to make more decisions, have more options?

The answer, according to most forms of psychotherapy, schools of philosophy, and social thinking, would be a resounding *Yes.* Or better put, the answer would seem to be a "spontaneous" *Of course!*

Because the thrust of most of the systems (including the religious) under which we have been brought up states that we have free will—which means that we can window-shop among the infinite alternatives of life, consciously, in an informed way, and choose the best path for ourselves. In many schools of therapy, the ability to pick and choose is an absolute indication of mental health. In most religions, as we know them, free will is exercised by following the particular path of the creed—and when we commit sins, we *choose* to, via our God-given capacity for free will.

In short, it is widely held that the sign of a person functioning without severe strains and burdens of neurosis is the person who can make choices. He or she is supposed to be free.

Therefore all of us, at some time or another, have considered ourselves to be neurotic or damaged or in pain because we have felt boxed in and have felt very keenly the suffering in being unable to make choices. We see others as having a world of choices especially when we feel stuck and weighed down. When we are immersed in a position of "I can't," we might even be convinced that we are the only unfree thing in the universe—that even lunatic asylums are filled with crazy but "happy" people. Or we say that *nobody* is free, and fall back into the cynical, pessimistic position—the position of passivity.

And when boxed and penned in, we've all thought that we have no choices at all, and never will have; that we can't work our way out of anything. And we think—and think.

The reason that we can't seem to dig our way out of this mess is that all this talk of free will and choice as being the great indicators of emotional health and freedom is simply another kind of fiction, another kind of illusion. It becomes circular—just like misapplied thinking.

Because *choosing* is always based on *thinking*—and as we noted before, thinking often has no place when we are dealing with emotional stuff.

Let's get into this.

If we ever have to make a choice about anything emotional, about anything that involves the larger concept of the soul, if we need to sift through alternatives in order to make a *correct*, a *right*, a *proper* choice—then that very process indicates that conflict still exists. We are not flowing reflexively. We are thinking again, and we need to make a choice that we *think* is "right," that we *think* might get us something or keep us out of trouble.

Any time we have to pause, think, wonder about what choice to make, we are right then in conflict, we are right then not free—and the choice we then make is not going to make us any freer. Because the same situation is going to occur again—and we will be faced with a "choice" again, the same conflict again.

On the other hand, freedom, the connection of the soul, is felt and expressed precisely when there is no choice at all. Not when the thinking apparatus can't come up with an answer and feels trapped—but when there is no choice about what you do, when the mind, body, soul are so fused together that our action is fluid, reflexive, and we do what must be done. With the ease of a flow that goes straight to the heart of the situation. Action that is perfect: that can't be described in any other way than absolute, perfect, not produced by thinking but as if all the pieces and parts suddenly, by themselves, become welded into a complete whole. Like building a boat of perfect dimensions and weight, a boat exactly fitted and equipped and weighted for the stream into which you place it. And when placed, its perfect dimensions in its perfect stream give the sense of total movement with no fight or struggle against waves or currents.

Absolute perfection of action. Absolute soul.

It's possible.

But before I say more about this, how we can try to achieve it, it's important to anticipate and clear up a question that may be rising to the surface right now.

Am I talking about blind action? Just doing something off the top of our heads? Plunging into something like a bull in a china shop regardless of who or what we hurt? Am I talking about behavior that psychotherapists call "acting out" or impulsivity?

Absolutely not: the bull in the china shop is just as unaware and unconscious as the person who labors an emotional situation to death with thinking.

I am not advocating that if you are angry at your boss, you walk into his office, hit him, and get fired and sued. And not that if you find yourself displeased or disappointed by your husband or wife, you just pack a bag and walk out. And also not that you march off to get killed in a war because you hear a Sousa march and watch a parade.

I am talking about balance. *Sheer balance.* Such a perfect, rhythmic, soul-connected balance that the right thing will be done at the right time without any thought whatever, without any struggle at all.

Sheer balance. The total rightness, fit, of balanced reflexiveness. The second nature that flows completely from the soul.

Much of what follows has been crystallized for me by a close colleague, and I want to start with an illustration that fits the incredible scope of the concept. It came straight from the soul, in one of those unguarded open moments in which truth is seen clearly.

Near the end of World War II, guards in the Nazi concentration camps were, regardless of their ages, being released from their duties to be sent to the front lines because the German army was becoming decimated by the Allies. In efforts to keep "order," some of the physically healthier prisoners were given a "choice": they could either pick up the departing guards' clubs and use them on their fellow prisoners, or they could remain in their state of terror and starvation.

The prisoners fell into three groups: those who willingly picked up the truncheons as a matter of self-preservation; those who felt the agony of the "choice" and who felt the need to think about it; and those who, without a thought or a moment's hesitation, said no. Said No, you will have to continue starving and beating me, but I can't torment or kill others.

And that's the heart of it. That's the kind of action we're interested in. That kind of connection, that kind of emergence of the soul. No thought of self-preservation, no thought of being beaten—no thought at all. Just the reflexive action that underlines the vast, powerful connection of everything with everything.

Absolute perfection of action.

No choice.

Total health.

Soul.

Obviously those who couldn't act so directly from the soul can hardly be condemned. They did what they *had* to do, and we all often do what he *have* to do. Let's also suspend any idea we might have that the people who said no were insane, self-destructive, or plainly suicidal.

Let's just see it as it is: the reflexive inability to be less than human, less than *fully* human. And that is one definition of the soul.

THE INNER PRISON

It works the same way inside us in situations far less openly powerful, far less frightening and stark—but no less dehumanizing. We frequently find ourselves trapped in some kind of interior prison in which we are supposed to make the proper choices, the right choices—and within our own small world we invariably see these situations as matters of life and death. Life and death, and we lose the Now.

Reflexive action, action flowing from soul-connection, always takes place in the now, because now is immediately, instantaneously seen and understood as important—as the only time that has meaning. Now is alive, while the past is dead and the future is somewhere off in the unknown— and so is just as dead.

If we know what is happening now, the future is of absolutely no importance. For example, many people who rely upon Astrology or Tarot cards solely to "tell the future" do so because they have no consciousness of the present. They don't know what is happening right now.

Again, I want to stress that this kind of action, which *has* to take place in the now, the now of spontaneity, is very different from the impulsive and often destructive activity that also *seems* to take place in the now.

Except that this kind of blind activity doesn't *ever* take place in the now—simply because this impulsive blindness is *always* a way of escaping from something. For instance, a person has a string of impulsive sexual encounters without intimate meaning or contact. Look even lightly and it will come out that he or she is trying to escape from a bad marriage—or even trying to escape from intimacy itself. So there is no connection with now: escape is running away from now. There is escapist activity in any situation which won't be faced—a situation which can *only* be faced in the now, whether a bad marriage or a fear of closeness.

To face ourselves, we must face ourselves *now*. There

is no other way. There is no future about this. You do it now or you don't do it at all.

Now is alive. You can only be reflexive *now*, only *now* can the soul emerge in relation to ourselves or others.

Now is a time of total responsibility. It has nothing to do with pleasure or with dropping out.

And to avoid now is to avoid life. We can only *live* now. Not yesterday and not tomorrow.

That's why, when we gain respect for the living moment, the idea of choice makes no sense. "If . . . then" has no place in the present. Only when we gain respect for ourselves as fully alive in *this* moment, as beings with soul and self-trust, does choice become irrelevant. And I am obviously not talking about choices that turn on what to eat for supper. I am talking only about the inner connection.

So how can we discover the Now? What do we do about that? Where is it? How do we feel and sense it?

Like the cigarette that we can't give up because we have never really had the experience of it, but have just smoked it so automatically that it has become a habit of which we aren't truly aware, we might start by paying attention to a process inside us.

EXPLORATION: Sit quietly, with as little external distraction as possible. Call to mind some things about which you feel you must make a choice. Don't necessarily think of something that you feel is deeply troubling you, don't label it that way. You don't have to look for big or small, less or more, because *anything* you feel you have to make a choice about is the problem, *is* troubling you, no matter how trivial it seems. Focus on anything that comes up; it doesn't matter.

Now that you've settled on a few situations, sift all the alternatives you can think of through your head—the positives, the negatives, the pros and cons.

You should feel yourself doing this very automatically because that's how we've been trained to do it, by raking through as many alternatives we can think of.

Once you feel you've exhausted the list, get a piece of paper and a pencil and make an actual list of the pros and cons—the situation itself, what you think will happen if you do what you want to (positive), what will happen if you do what you feel you should (negative). Write it out in three columns.

Like as not you will still be in the same dilemma, right? Except now you can see it all in front of you. And a theme should begin to emerge very clearly: making a positive choice, while it may get you something you want, is being blocked by some sort of fear or guilt or both. Go ahead, label it: fear of what, guilt about what? What are you afraid of or guilty about that *hasn't happened yet*—that you can't be sure will happen because you can't predict the future?

Just simply see how predictions based upon thinking can stop you. How *sure* you might "feel" about an uncertain future. How *sure* you might "feel" about how another person *might* react. See how you are speaking for that person—as if you are *telling* him or her how to react.

And you will see that your necessity for choice has nothing to do with what *is*, but with what you think *might be*.

THE FEAR OF NOW

What happens here is that we become afraid of the now (again, there *cannot* be an intellectual choice in the matter of reflexiveness) and plummet backward into some vague future. We use that future precisely to obscure our possibilities. Preoccupation with the future, with a time that hasn't happened, and preoccupation with the past, which is dead, totally destroys our capacity to flow, to connect with the energy of the soul.

So therefore we *think* that some choice is necessary.

And many of us would like to have the problem solved *for* us. We might ask a friend, a parent, go to a counselor, get mad at our therapists because they can't solve the thing. Not won't, but *can't*.

No one can solve the problem.

No one can solve the problem because there is no problem. But we like to label the nonproblem as an inability to make a choice.

And then we think we're neurotic.

THE SÉANCE

We were sitting in a circle, some fifteen or twenty of us, students and supervisors participating in a demonstration of psychodrama—a technique in which people act the roles of their conflicts and the figures important in them. At one point we were asked to recount a past memory— any memory that occurred to us, pleasant, unhappy, whatever it might be.

The vast majority of the memories were ones from early life, and almost all were painful. All these thoughts, these memories, filled the already dimly lit room with deep gloom—and it was hard to tell if these were "real" memories or distorted perceptions of important people, important places. All psychotherapists recognize that memories almost never rise in pure, "as-it-really-was" form. Our memories don't work that way: they are usually bits and pieces of accuracy mixed with fantasy and stirred with thoughts.

But everyone in that room, with the exception of one person, thought his memory was "true." Believed it—and became saddened by it.

I had the sense of sitting in a séance. Not because the lights were dimmed or because we were all holding hands—although this contributed a bit to the effect.

It was a séance because we were summoning up the dead—trying to raise the dead with our thoughts. Trying, and succeeding, to live in the past. Had we stayed there long enough, night after night, I am convinced that we would finally have produced something like the group in Canada that Lyall Watson described. We would have produced a Philip. We would have materialized a fiction.

And we actually do that when we live in the past: the semifictional people in our past gain "real" identity; they may not knock over a table or chase someone around a room, but they become just as powerful within us. They become our pursuers and our jailers.

All those students, their supervisors, after so many years of personal psychotherapy and psychoanalysis, were still living in the past, among the dead. *Now* did not exist in that room.

And no one questioned it at all.

And, usually, neither do any of us no matter where we are.

Not if we conduct our lives like a séance.

EXPLORATION: Take your list and look at it again. Look at the situation, then at the positive side, the I-want-to, I'd-like-to side. Now look at the negatives across the way. For example, the positive statement, "I would like to tell off my boss" might be opposed by, "But he will fire me" or some other variation. "I would like to get out of my bad marriage" might, as its opposite, have "But I can't wreck a home, I can't hurt my husband/wife, I can't abandon my kids."

In there, in that list, is contained some form of reflexive action. Some of these positives are going to be negatively phrased, such as the ones above: "I would like to tell off my boss," "I would like to get out of my bad marriage." Turn them now into more positive statements that lurk just below the surface: "I would like to be more assertive with my boss, I would like to let him know that I am a person with dignity"; "I would like to have a good, fulfilling relationship with a man/woman."

Now pair up the rearranged positives with the negatives:

"I would like to be more assertive with my boss, I would like to let him know that I am a person with dignity."

vs.

"But he will fire me."

Or:

"I would like to have a good, fulfilling relationship with a man/woman."

vs.

"But I can't wreck a home, I can't hurt my husband/wife, I can't abandon my kids."

Let this sink in for a minute or two.

So what holds you back from presenting yourself as, or demanding if necessary, that you are a person with dignity? How does your wish to have a fulfilling relationship threaten to hurt or destroy another person, your children?

What is it that you're waiting for to put these things into effect? You were predicting dire results based on negative propositions—and *that's* the trouble, at least part of it. Cast your wants in positive, moving, alive ways and there will be far less trouble.

The reason we get stuck in this matter of choices is that we often put the I-want-to action in terms of anger, escape, frustration, and then wedge it into some false image of low self-esteem and self-worth, some future expectation of pain or punishment. And we do this because we are "active" a lot like the frustrated kids that we once were, *and we were kids in the past.* So of course our thoughts will go to the future, into another "dead" time, and we will envision some punishment or bad situation we had or think we had in the past. My boss will fire me the same as somebody back in the past tried to block me when I was assertive. (If we are afraid to be assertive, we will invariably become angry.)

Will your boss really fire you if you present yourself positively, without anger, without the frightened approach that comes from anxiety? You must be worth *something* to the company; if not, why haven't you been fired already? To have a home wrecked by wanting love and fulfillment, to have people reject you for that wish, to feel you will hurt someone by that very human want—well, I leave it to your imagination about what might have happened back then in the past. We will have a lot of work to do to overcome *that* fear.

What we are doing in this Exploration is taking a *situation* that seems concrete and translating it into a character trait—something that is deep within us, not at the surface of a cause-and-effect isolated "problem."

See how the Now is murdered? The future is the past. And the living moment of soul-connection is aborted. Choice—the necessity for it and the conflict that surrounds it—is a way of living in the past.

EXPLORATION: Take a final look at the list. See some really positive statements that you don't have to *turn around* into positives. This list should be a little easier to deal with now that you have worked with the more complicated positives and negatives. Action here, reflexive action, might now be simpler, more in the spotlight. Sometimes we have to get at the more hidden layers of things before the more obvious ones are clear to us. Let's use statements similar to the ones above for purposes of clarity.

I want a raise.

vs.

My boss will say no.

I would like to date that woman/man.

vs.

She'll say no. He'll think I'm too aggressive if I approach him.

I want a better marriage.

vs.

It's no use trying. It's hopeless.

Now what do we have here? Three possibilities out of thousands, again all perfectly legitimate desires, very meaningful desires, and all countered by thoughts that the wants will be thwarted. Of course the negatives stem from a variety of thoughts:

1. My desires are *not* legitimate and so are com-

pletely dependent on what the other person does
or says;

2. Social conditioning defines male/female roles and
so "prevents" connected action;

3. *Any* sort of communication is difficult, perhaps
even impossible;

4. The other person wants to deprive me;

5. I'm involved with monsters.

If we cut it to the bone, all these blocks (*out there*)
to what I want are the creations of thought and thinking—
thinking either based on what other people believe and
say, on our own fears, or on some past experience that we
have rooted into and carry around with us as if one
particular situation means that all situations have to be
identical. For example, everybody in the office says that the
boss doesn't give raises. Or, in the past I have been turned
down for a raise. Or even that nobody would ever give
me candy when I asked for it.

So we are not going to get on with it in the present
because of somebody else's useless, dead information,
or because some place in the past we have had a bad experience that we keep on using to stop our movement.

So we will try to make a "choice." With the boss we
will try to build a case for why we are entitled to a raise—
completely forgetting, as I've mentioned, that if we hadn't
been doing good work we'd have been fired or warned
already. Grasping at the thought of the depriving boss (a
thought converted into a "reality"), we will build a case
based on all the reasons for which we think we deserve
the raise. What will begin to happen in the construction
of this list is that we will begin to sense a growing anger,
an anger hooked to the idea that we are having to defend
ourselves against the Big No. Then we are hopelessly

trapped in anger, creating a list that has no meaning or impact, setting up a powerful antagonism between ourselves and the boss—and then we make the "choice" of either walking into his office, presenting the case while enraged underneath—or declining altogether with the statement, "I can't. It's useless. He'll just say 'no.' "

Why not just ask for the raise and see what happens on the spot?

We look at these authority people as if they are a mother or father who is going to tell us that we can't have the candy. The "mature" list of deserving reasons is just an adult variation on telling our parents that we have cleaned our rooms, brushed our teeth, said our prayers. And now can we have the candy? The ice cream? The toy?

We assume that people in higher positions are antagonists, including spouses, whom we also tend to place in higher positions. And we waste boundless time and energy working within the rigid confines of that system. Instead of using the energy to live and connect with ourselves, we pour it down the drain, trapping it inside us in the form of anger and frustration.

A client tells me the story—a joke—about a man whose car has a flat tire at three o'clock in the morning. He has a jack but no tire iron, there are no gas stations open, so he decides to find the nearest house and ask for help. He ruminates on the lateness of the hour as he walks on, begins to think about how he'll be received when he rings the doorbell: whoever answers will be angry at being awakened, might be frightened, might even be violent, might be some cheap bastard who hates people, a sadist. He thinks all this as he walks on, seeing it very vividly in his thoughts, seeing the person slam the door in his face, screaming at him—and finally he gets to a house and, already toweringly angry because of his thoughts, rings the doorbell. When the person answers, our man, livid with the anger stoked up by his thoughts, shouts at the sleepy face: "Take your tire iron and shove it!"

We get nothing from building the case—except the repeated depressing thought that we must jump through hoops for anything we want. And then *that* thought devastates our self-esteem. Finally, even the raise itself gets to be soured because we had to humiliate ourselves for it.

And we lose something vital to us: we don't get the sense that our whole being simply flows in, asks for the raise, and gets it. We get no sense that our connectedness, our self-worth, has produced it. We just have the rotten feeling that we've begged like an undeserving child.

You can apply what we are beginning to learn in any encounter simply by remembering that every situation is new—by being aware of that. *That no matter what has happened in the past, no matter what we've heard from other people, it doesn't hold true in the present and has nothing to do with you.*

There is no choice.

Just find out for yourself. And then you will know —but remember too that you will know something only about that time, that place, that situation, that person. It may not apply at all in the future.

That is how to grab the Now.

The rest is illusion, and illusion is something we don't want to build a life on.

We can only experience, learn, something now—otherwise we will live in fear always. Life, situations, instead of being what they are, will be like hot stoves that we have to avoid touching.

So doing it now also means giving up self-protection

—which is so much of what all this useless thinking is about—and we will soon get very deeply into that.

If we do these explorations into ourselves and see how the thoughts of *what might happen* prevent us from connecting with ourselves and using the energy within—if we do them with awareness, we will see what stops us. If we open to them and see ourselves honestly, without justifying anything, without accusing something *out there* of stopping us, then we can see the control and force we give up, hand over. We will see that our *I can'ts* are not products of what is *real now*, but are based on air, on thoughts, on fantasy.

It's like the parable of the two men who, long ago, were walking barefoot along a hard, rough road. One man said:

"Wouldn't it be wonderful if this road, from where we started to where we are going, were paved with nice soft leather?"

The other said nothing, but fell into his imagination. They parted at a crossroads and never saw each other again.

For the rest of his life the first man dreamed of leather-paved roads.

The other man invented shoes.

THE LEATHER-PAVED ROAD

Therapists see this all the time. A client will experience tremendous anxiety because he or she wants to tell something about their life but is afraid and ashamed to—and the shame is often connected to fears of what the therapist, the *out there,* will say; but more deeply it is connected to a panic in admitting something to oneself in an open committed way. And then, when the "secret" comes out, there is a funny, trembly moment of complete confusion—because nothing horrible has happened. The therapist is not turned off, and the client has stopped lying to him or herself. And then so much begins to open; so much energy begins to flow—so much begins to be expressed from the soul which has been freed from its trap of thoughts. Like the shoes, the soul suddenly seems "invented."

All the boss can do is say no. Or yes.

If the woman or man declines your request for a date, it may be her or his problem. But without the risk of a no, there can be no possibility of a yes.

If your husband or wife won't cooperate with you in trying to create a better marriage—either by talking together or seeking professional help, or by taking any kind of mutual responsibility for the bad situation—then you will *know* that the marriage is no good. You won't just brood on it. You might escape a wallow of self-pity.

And here's an important point, a crucial point. If you come to *know* that the marriage is no good, that it is destructive to you—then what choice can you possibly make if you are to grow as a *fully human person?* What choice can there possibly be? What choice if—again—you are to grow and realize that you have a soul, a great depth?

There is no choice.

You leave. Not because you are selfish, but because you have tried to explore ways of making the thing better, have gotten no cooperation, and no longer want to maintain a state of living decay.

It is not selfish to grow. Growth is the only thing there is.

It is selfish *not* to leave, *not* to grow: it traps the other person in his or her own deadness and childishness; it scars your children beyond belief to live in a house with a broken spirit and a rage of resentment radiating in the very walls. It is a rationalizing trick of thinking that children can't see the bitterness; and what you will teach them is how not to grow, how not to grow by clinging to relationships that offer only neurotic security.

If we must think of others, why can't we think in terms of their *freedom*?

Your growth, your happiness, spreads. The selfishness of nongrowth, the turning from your own soul, drags you down along with everyone around you.

And we must realize one thing: if we make a "choice" (which is no real choice at all, but the kind of false choice we have been indoctrinated to make) to stay in a deadening situation, then in full honesty with ourselves we must admit that we are not being concerned with others at all—again, "My wife will crack up or commit suicide if I leave," "My kids will be products of a broken home" (a home is people, and only *they* can be broken or whole) —but are being concerned only with ourselves. We are dependent on the others and have it twisted around to make them dependent on us—and justify it with grandiose thoughts that they will crack up without us. As a client put it, when gaining insight into a dependent relationship in which she appeared to be dominant: "My dependency is that I want him to be dependent on *me*."

All this means is that we are afraid to be free. And we, each of us, must face that—if it is true. *That is how we live in the now.*

EXPLORATION: Now simply make a list of all the

things you feel will contribute to your growth, to your in-touchness, to the unfolding of your soul. Now oppose them with what you think stands in your way.

Whatever stands in the way of your growth is destructive. Not *whoever,* but *whatever.* And the whatever is probably your thoughts.

Now find a way to get rid of this "whatever"—not by attacking it with an emotional hatchet, by being destructive yourself, but just by ignoring it, by passing *through* it, in favor of doing what it is that will help you grow. If another person is involved, deepen yourself before you tend to attack. Discover what *you* lack before demanding that someone else fill your space.

And then there is no anger in it, there is no enemy. There is just your soul.

Let's, for a moment, ponder this:

A client of mine "felt" utterly trapped by her father, who typically responded to her every independent movement by complaining of severe pains in his chest. My client was completely convinced that unless she fell in with her father's demands, he would die of a heart attack. She *believed* this—despite family knowledge that once, checking out his chest pain after my client decided to take her own apartment (she was twenty-six), he received a clean bill of health.

She understood fully that he was manipulating her, but she believed that he was using a *real* heart condition as the weapon. She could not believe that it could all be just a ploy.

So she sat in her new apartment, alone, going back to her family every time her father summoned her for dinner, visits, whatever, always cajoling her to return, warning her that she would get a reputation of a "bad" girl. She was just as trapped in her apartment as she had been at home—perhaps even more so because his attacks were all the more relentless now that she was somewhat removed from the family scene.

And then the irony.

She could no longer stand the strain and decided that she would move back home.

It was a Saturday night. She sat at the table eating dinner with her father, mother, and two younger sisters; and feeling as if she were dying, yet having to die, she said:

"I'm giving up the apartment. I'm coming back home to live."

"Ah," her father said, "you've come to your senses."

"I guess," she answered.

"Either you guess or you have—which is it?"

"Yes, I have."

"So you'll admit I was right all the time?"

And then, what she described as going down for the third time:

"Yes. You were right all the time."

"Good. That's good."

He seemed elated. He actually rubbed his hands together. She felt dead.

After supper she went up to her old room to spend the night, and as she sat on the edge of her bed, looking out through her window into the darkness, wondering what other people, couples, were doing on this Saturday night—her mother suddenly rushed into the room, trying to scream, but her voice stifled so that the sound came out in eerie squeaks. She went out with her mother into her parents' bedroom—and sprawled across the bed was her father clutching at his chest, breathing in heavy rasping gasps, then wildly flailing his arms.

An ambulance came and took him to the hospital.

By noon the next day he was dead.

When she sat with me in the session she told me that she had cried a great deal, but she had a perfect understanding then that she had had nothing to do with his heart attack.

"I did what he wanted," she said, "and he died anyway." Then: "Thank God. Thank God I'm only twenty-six."

7
Self-Image: Is It Real?

"SOMETHING" MUST DIE

"I'm sitting in a chapel. I can see it's dimly lit, with candle-light flickering on the walls, and it's very solemn. A little way in front of me is a coffin, and it's raised a bit, up on the steps, and I'm sitting in a pew so I can't see who's in it. I'm aware that I want to see who's in it, but I'm very afraid to stand up and look. But it's like a magnet—I *have* to look. I have to see what's there. It's important. So I stand, walk up a little, and look inside.

"God! It's me. It's me, lying there dead. I have a terrible feeling of panic, and yet suddenly there isn't any panic. I can't say it better. I'm afraid and I'm not. I know the dream went on further, but I can't remember any more of it."

This is Mark. He has been telling me this dream about seeing himself dead—and it is a dream that has frightened clients, therapists, and people who have never set foot in a therapist's office.

But why be frightened by what you don't know? To stop fear you go into it.

He knows that the dream went on, but he can't recollect the rest of it. Where does it go? What has died?

He relaxes himself, closes his eyes, becomes calm, and places himself back in his dream, standing before the coffin, and begins to visualize, then describe, what he sees and feels.

"The face is mine, all right, but it's set tight, unpleasant—no, I know what it looks like. It looks scared, like it's been scared and has tightened up as if it's afraid to get hit. No one else would know that except me, though. Only I know what's behind that mask. Anyone else seeing it would just think it's a rigid person, a judgmental kind of person—haughty. That's it; that's it completely. A haughty, rigid, put-downish kind of person. But *I* can see through that. . . . Funny, it looks like the embalmer made him up to look that way. I can see beneath the makeup. A scared person who wears some kind of mask the undertaker gave him.

"I close the lid. There's no reason to keep looking. And then I turn around and walk away, walk out of that chapel. I'm going through the door now. . . . Jesus! There's a beach. I turn around but the chapel is gone, and all I can see is this beautiful beach, white, sloping down to the surf, and the water is all kinds of blue and green, as far as I can see. I run, clothes and all, straight down the beach and into the water. I'm in the surf now and it's sparkly and cool and alive. . . ."

He becomes a dolphin, a shark, a whale, a small fish playing through the surf. He becomes himself and lets the water, the flow of it, take him where it will—because the water is inside, it is himself, and he is letting himself take him where he will. . . .

Something has died.

And something is being born.

SELF-ESTEEM

So far we've gone through a lot together—on a different kind of journey, one in which we've been examining our usual ways of looking at things—ways we've been taught are "reality," as the way life is. And we've been questioning that directly.

We've looked at thoughts, we've seen how they can create a whole unreal world, we see how they stand in the way of our flow, our soul, in the way of reflexive right action.

So if thoughts—where they are not used properly—can create our fears, then thoughts can also create our own self-images. Because self-images are what we think about ourselves—and almost never what we truly are, what is real. Remember my cousin Lucy, the little girl who had the thought—but not her own experience—that kids will take advantage of a "too-nice" teacher? We speculated on how she could carry that foreign, externally implanted belief into adulthood and build part of her life around it. Let's go after the big fish now—the whole thing, the whole "I," the whole "Ego"—that thing we build our identities around, the vehicle we take an "ego trip" in, that "thing" we think gives us a feeling of separate boundaries, a sense of individualism whether "rugged" or not. Let's see how we protect it at all costs.

Our Explorations here may be scary. If they are, we

will stay with the fright. They may also be gateways to joy, gateways to the soul. We will stay with that as well.

At first all of it shook me to the roots.

I'm glad it did.

As with Mark, it *is* a little bit like dying before coming to life again. One goes with the other. There can be no death without a rebirth. No rebirth without death.

As we said before, there may be no such thing as low self-esteem, but that it might just be a thought or a set of related thoughts—deeply ingrained related thoughts that "feel" real. And self-esteem is part of a self-image; they are tightly tied together.

Let's suppose that someone carries around with him or her a self-*image* of being a very independent person: tough-minded, practical, intelligent, a "show-me" type. The person believes this image of himself, believes it is true, values it, believes it *is* him. Not only will he try to live his life based on this self-image—*but largely unknown to him,* he will have to spend a great deal of energy *protecting* the image. And he will protect it at any expense—because he *thinks* it is him, and so it will be terribly important that he protect *himself.*

Protect himself against what?

Against anything that in any way contradicts or threatens this image of himself that he thinks *is* himself.

He will be very alert to any clue that contradicts this image—no matter how "objective" it seems.

His base of operations will be the practical, everyday world of facts, figures, and masculine unsentimentality. (Women, too, can fall into a socially recognizable masculine role.) He will admit only hard data, evidence, into his life. He will not be able freely to express or even sense emotion in emotional situations. His approach to making love will be just as practical and unsentimental: he will appraise the female market like an investor. He will look for a wife in the same way: what practical "things" can she contribute to his life? Science and technology will be his sole guides in life; each new building, no matter how ugly, will be a sign of progress. He will read only what applies to his career. Art, beauty, will have no real place: he may master the history of painting but never stroll through a museum.

He believes that this is the right way to live, that he is right. And necessarily that others not like him are wrong. A style of survival, of life and death, of "them" and "us" is beginning to form, to be a way of life.

Yet he has no idea, no real awareness, that he has to protect this self-image of rightness all day, all month, all year, all life long.

When he puts down another man for being emotionally clobbered by a movie, he doesn't realize that he has been threatened by a display of feeling in another man—because men debate, analyze, not feel. When he appraises a woman for her utility, he doesn't realize that he is afraid of intimate relationships. When he is not at all responsive to music (although he might have a status subscription to the Metropolitan Opera), he is not aware that some deep creative spark has all but gone out inside him.

If he felt any of this, if he admitted to any of it, he would be consumed by anxiety and depression, and he would become terribly frightened, feeling that he had fallen into some sort of abyss.

Because admitting these feelings would be threatening to his self-image—to himself, ultimately to his idea of himself. And so he keeps every conflicting possibility out of his awareness in order to protect this self-image.

He doesn't know who he is.

He talks of a life-style.

Never of a life *content*.

All he is, is a set of ideas, a set of thoughts. He has very little reality of his own. He lives as a reflection of the images and ideas of others—his parents, society, culture. But there is nothing individual about him. He doesn't know that he is a bundle of walking clichés.

He will debate anything, argue anything, that threatens this self-image.

We see this all the time: two people going at it tooth and nail—about an interpretation of a movie, a play, a book, politics. They are in no way looking for the truth, or even to learn something: they are protecting their self-images and so they are protecting what they think is themselves, their identities.

That's why these quarrels have a life-and-death quality to them. The issue is survival. The soul can't play free in this field.

Let's stress it again, because we all, at some time or another, engage in this kind of thing.

In a quarrel, it always seems that something objective is being debated—because one needs some sort of neutral area to maintain the illusion that no death struggle is going on. So we pick a play, an election. Quickly the argument becomes a quarrel and sometimes even a fight. It is very obvious that no play, no election, is being fought over.

It may not be so obvious that what is taking place is a fight for sheer survival—a struggle not as direct as that in the jungle (or the streets of the South Bronx) where actual territory and physical life are at stake, but a fight for the survival of what one thinks is one's identity and consequently one's whole existence.

There is really no other root way to account for this phenomenon. It is a fight to the death—to victory or defeat.

The person who is defeated in this quarrel invariably becomes depressed, even sick, after the anger subsides; depressed, perhaps very nervous, physically ill. Perhaps all three.

Because his self-image, as he thinks of it, has been murdered—and he suddenly feels that he doesn't know who he is any more. This can scare the hell out of anyone.

So two people who are fighting over what seems to be a neutral event, really fighting, can be said to have shaky senses of identity and self-image. A self-image based on thoughts and not a sense of self based on self-knowledge. This is always a shaky proposition. You can't build a house on air. And we have all had this experience in greater or lesser degrees.

If we are thinking of our own self-images at this point, let's try not to get too upset or defensive. If we do, we might be laboring under a self-image, part of which is that our self-image is terrific and stable and sound, that is—*real*. Try to let go of it for a minute: we're all in the same boat. We lose our real sense of ourselves, lose the sense of soul, beneath these images that are only products of our thinking.

What is being played out in these encounters with others is the protection of the self-image—*as if it is real,* as if it is really what makes us full human beings, persons, keeps us alive. We are protecting an illusion, a fantasy— and that becomes very obvious when, say, the battle leaves the field of the play and slides into the fight. Someone, maybe even yourself, is going to say: "Why are you taking this so personally?" And there it is.

This question has to be asked by *ourselves*. It usually

comes from an outsider—who will then go off and get engaged in his own identity struggle with someone else.

The question *must* be asked of ourselves.

Why *do* we take these things so personally? Why am I willing to spoil a whole evening by a fight over some external event? Of what importance is the play to me, *past* what enjoyment or message I derived from it?

It seems that most of our waking lives are spent in a position of defense. We seem to be least defended when we sleep, when our inner life can breathe easier and begin, via dreams, to give us real messages about ourselves. We communicate to ourselves better, more honestly, in our dreams, even though the images often seem weird and unfathomable —and later we are going to see how we can make our dreams work for us in waking life.

What we are defending is a self-image, or a cluster of them, and none of it is real at all.

In psychotherapy, therapists get to points of terrific pain and confusion with certain clients—and they usually refer to this as being "stuck." They look for hidden personal feelings toward the client—feelings that may be stopping progress; they also look for "resistances" in the clients. But very often nothing seems to work, and this stuckness goes on until something lucky happens to free it up, or the client leaves, or the therapist openly admits he or she is stuck—or everything just stops dead.

After years of doing therapy and supervising students at all levels of training, I have come to see that what is really happening here is this:

The client has a particular self-image, perhaps a very special one, a deep one that isn't very apparent on the surface. The process of therapy has brought the situation to the point of a threat to this self-image and the client begins his life-or-death struggle to protect it. The therapist, on the other hand, really doesn't see this self-image, let alone understand it; but what he dimly knows is that his *own* self-image (the competent, knowledgeable, skilled therapist, and therefore the worthwhile mature person) is being very badly threatened by the protective efforts of the client. In short, he can't get through the client's protective armor—and finds himself then needing to protect his own self-image of the competent therapist.

So now you have both client and therapist protecting themselves, protecting their threatened self-images and consequently what they think are their identities. So of course nothing is going to happen. What is in that room is sheer illusion—nothing. Two people protecting fantasies, two people, each not wanting to be wiped out by the other.

We do this all the time, one with another.

And it is all total illusion.

EXPLORATION: Right now, let's see if we're involved in this illusion together.

How are you thinking about what I've just said? Catch your thoughts. See what they are saying to you. List them. See if you can place a feeling next to each one: anger, satisfaction, annoyance, joy, whatever.

See what feelings are being triggered off by your thoughts.

What are you thinking about *me?* List these thoughts too; and fill in the feelings that go with them.

Maybe you're even thinking that my, or part of my, self-image is very involved in getting these ideas through to you. That my sense of identity rests on a conception of myself as a person who has the answers and wants to tell you that you don't. That I'm right and you're wrong.

But the most important thing you can do right now is

to sense in yourself how you are looking at this—if you are feeling positively or negatively emotional. If so, there is something within you that feels it needs protection. If the ideas are bothering you and you feel negatively toward them, see what it is you're protecting.

Do you think that I might be attacking you with the accusation that your life is wrong? A fake? An Illusion?

Just list the thoughts, the feelings, the sense of it.

Right now I am of no importance whatever. I have no identity. Make it a one-party interaction. See how *you* think, *you* feel.

If I am hanging *my* self-image on whether you accept these ideas or not, then *I* am in trouble, and *I* will have to take care of that.

I continue to make my own lists.

GETTING THROUGH THE IMAGES

To get through my self-image is to get deeper, to get closer to my soul—to shed the thoughts that build my shaky identity so that I can find out truly who I am and live a life of spontaneity, reflexive action, and responsibility. But I have to shed the thoughts that form the illusion of my identity.

You might say: But I *feel* that way, I *feel* I am so and so, I don't have the sense of *thinking* it.

Far too often we're usually not aware of *thinking* it. To repeat, what happens during our many years of dependent childhood is that our heads are filled with the thoughts, beliefs, commands of others. And if we are the targets of a large batch of negative thoughts repeated over and over, they form a cluster, a group. We then think that our "goodness" or "badness" depend on them. Our self-images become formed by this cluster or group of thoughts.

Then all we need later on is a thought, any thought in the cluster, and it immediately produces the bad feeling, which we will do anything to get away from before seeing that it is based on a thought, or nothing. But the thought comes so close to the feeling it produces that we don't immediately catch the thought. Looking at it from a different angle, the gap between the thought and the feeling is often too tiny to see.

It might *seem* that the feeling strikes first, but only because there is almost no time lag in this process. It happens in its own deadly reflexive way—just as someday, when the soul is free, the good feeling can be coupled on the spot to the good thought. And when that happens, there is no experience of the thought at all.

Let's draw one of the many possibilities. (See next page).

And so we have lost the ability to see that the thought caused the depression in the first place, based on information that had nothing to do with us, but only on what we've been told.

Of course in adult life a lot of criticism comes from outside people as it did in childhood—and usually we will react badly to it just as we did long ago. But we have to see that no one really has the power that our parents *actually* had—and that *here and now* it is our thoughts that trigger the same old bad feelings. *The original powers are gone. We are no longer dependent children.*

The same diagram holds true for any self-image that is based on a cluster of thoughts. The one we drew leads to the self-image: *I am a bad and worthless person and I don't deserve anything.* Or it can lead to an allied self-

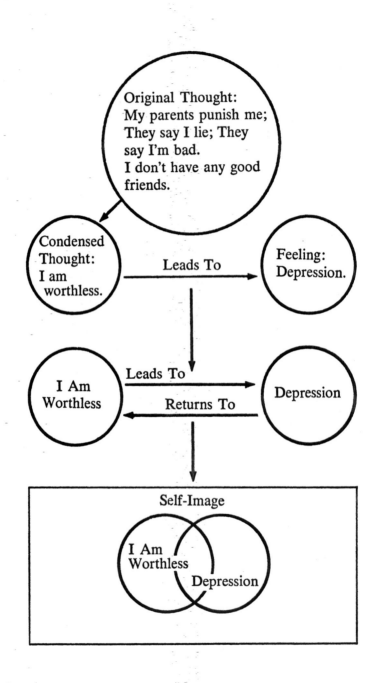

image of: *I am a hard, tough person, and nothing will ever hurt me again*—an image created to prevent the pain of "feeling" worthless. They overlap—and are produced by the thoughts.

So the thoughts are what we have to get rid of so that we can stop torturing ourselves, stop being guilty, stop living behind masks that always need protection. When the negative thoughts are stopped, the painful feelings are stopped as well.

Don't forget that *any* self-image built on these illusions of thinking has to be protected—no matter how positively or negatively these images are seen by oneself or the public.

Abandoning the self-protection is a way to get at shedding the false self-image. And here might be the scary part—the scary *thought:* But if my self-image is an illusion, has no reality to it, *What will I have left if I drop it?*

Yourself.

Who you really are.

The richness of your inner life.

Your soul.

But you must shed the skin easily, gently, step-by-step, and at your own proper pace—so that as the illusion begins to drop away you can slowly get to see that the real you is not a bad person, not an uptight bundle of defensiveness; that you are much more feeling than you might have thought, much more sympathetic, relaxed, imaginative, spontaneous—and ultimately creative.

It can still be a bit scary because you might also find out that you're not as hard as you thought, or as tough—that you're softer, more open (*not* "vulnerable"), more emotional, that you've been "wrong" about a lot of things because of the self-protectiveness.

Only in a state of openness can we live fully and experience our souls.

"Vulnerability" is the negative social word used to avoid openness and taking chances.

You'll *feel* life more deeply—its joys and sorrows. Because the world will open more—because you will let it, not shutting out anything in order to play the deadly game of self-protection. Once you don't have to protect yourself, all things become possible because you will be letting anything that comes your way enter in. And things will become electrifyingly clear.

Want to go on?

EXPLORATION: Make a two-part list of your thoughts about yourself. One part, the positive thoughts; the other part, negative thoughts.

I stress lists because that way you can see things in front of you and avoid the tendency, as in our diagram, to have them run together in your head and thus form the two overlapping clouds trapped in the box. With a list you can see the incredible number of the thoughts, and so you can see the enormous number of possibilities for the self-image to be attacked or protected in a variety of situations, external and internal.

When you are sure that you've exhausted all the possibilities, all the thoughts, bracket them, by positive and negative, and across the way see if you can form them all, like pieces, into one or more self-images.

For example, in a shortened form:

Positive Thoughts	*Self-Image*
I'm often nice to others.	
I have a sense of humor.	I'm a pleasant, easy-to-
I'm not pushy.	get-along-with person.

Negative Thoughts	*Self-Image*
I don't like my looks.	
I often feel lonely.	Actually I'm often an
I don't express my anger.	unhappy person.

Now oppose the positive self-image or images with the negative ones and see what you get. In our short example, "I'm a pleasant, easy-to-get-along-with person" contrasts sharply, conflicts, with "I'm actually an often unhappy person." Here, one is the social front, the other the private thoughts, bad thoughts, about oneself. The secret negative image.

In this hypothetical list, the positive self-image is a positive social compensation for the negative one—which is private. That is, the outer mask for the negative inner image. So at all costs the secret stuff has to stay secret to protect the positive self-image. It will become desperately important that this person is never pushy, but bubbles with humor, etc., in order not to "feel" the threat of exposure of the inner image. For example, the secret anger and loneliness must stay hidden. The tension between these two, between the inner and the outer, can be almost unbearable.

If you are like most of us, you will find that the positive self-image, even if you believe in it, is the one that you usually try to present to the world, to the people you meet in it. Especially to those you think are "important," from whom you can get something you need or want—anything from affection to a job.

You will be hiding the negative self-image or images as well as you can, compensating for them, pretending they don't exist. You will be fragmenting yourself in this way, feeling terrible tension, not feeling together, not being able to be spontaneous.

Now comes an Exploration that requires a very direct self-confrontation.

EXPLORATION: List all the self-images you have come up with, and next to each one describe the ways you might have of protecting them, of reacting to "attacks" on them. Every way you can think of—because every way you can think of is a way you *have* used or *can* use. Stir your imagination. Get as wild as you want in order to see how far this business can go, what lies beneath the protection.

For example: I could kill anybody who calls me pushy.

That will clue you into how angry you really might be. Let it go, run wild with it. Be strong. Be totally ruthless with yourself if you can.

Even if you're getting a bit nervous about this self-confrontation, stick with it. Because you're already beginning to dent the images. The nervousness shows it: you're already moving from an old, stuck position, taking a chance on the unknown and doing it. And you're doing it *now*.

Below is a sample list, positive and negative. I give only one negative because this is a more complex area requiring more exploration later.

SELF-IMAGE

I am a bright well-read person.

PROTECTION

Since I can't admit socially that I haven't read some of the latest books without having this image shot down, I must:
1. Lie and say I've read what I haven't.
2. Avoid questions about new books.
3. Pretend I've been too busy to read.
4. Put down the unread book because the author's last one was "bad"—and steer the conversation to the last "bad" book.

I am cool, hip, with it, rational.

Showing excitement or being like anyone else blows the image. I must:
1. Be cynical about peak emotions.
2. Accuse others of being childish.
3. Try to act in a detached way.
4. Dismiss anything that is not "fact."
5. Appear to have "inside" information.
6. Drop names that no one has ever heard of.

SELF-IMAGE

I'm not liked. People walk away from me.

PROTECTION

The idea is to keep others away, even drive them away, to maintain this poor image (because I'm afraid of people). I must:

1. Talk too much; talk nonsense.
2. Say nothing at all.
3. Get drunk and slobbery.
4. Criticize anything and everything.
5. Ask blunt, direct personal questions without letting the other person "warm up" or know you.

Okay, now build your own list.

Something might come clear after you've finished. A kind of bonus. Not only will you see that a number of your self-images are shaky and need relatively constant protection (the main purpose of this Exploration), but you might have discovered one or two that require no protective efforts at all. Those are the "real" ones, the secure ones; and when you are putting them out naturally, with ease and without thinking or watching yourself going through the act, you do not experience discomfort, guardedness, or attack.

So you will have discovered something positive, something true and reflexive, about yourself.

Remember that the point of self-exploration is not a silly Horatio Alger-type of exercise in which you try to ferret out your "bad" traits or qualities in order to get rid of them by positive thinking, positive actions, or artificially reversing your behavior.

The point is to see what's there. To discover what is sound, solid, and energizing within you—so that you can feel the strength of your personality and its movement, and so discover the power and freedom of your soul. And remember that we are after *balance*—the negative *and* the positive. The imbalance, the blacks and whites, are what cause our problems, our one-sided idea that we haven't "got it together."

For example, a client of mine closes his eyes and lets himself visualize. At first everything is black, darkness, and suddenly a spider comes into view. It's huge, frightening, poised there in the darkness, the void. He erupts in a sweat and begins to tremble. I urge him to give the spider a place, a setting where spiders belong: spiders don't hover or lurk or float in pure dark space.

My client produces a web, then the fork of a tree, finally the whole tree. He materializes more trees, bushes, grass, flowers, a stream; the sun appears in a cloudless sky. And suddenly the spider is small, right-sized, a fleck of nature in its own natural setting. And it is no longer the least bit threatening or scary.

All things in their proper places.

When all things find their proper, natural places, the experience of fear is all but impossible. It's much more difficult to project our fear-producing thoughts into something with a context, something properly proportioned, than into something hanging in space, alone. Without a reference, without *relativity,* the spider was terrifying; in

its web, in a tree, in a country scene, it was ordinary, small
—in short just a spider.

It was what it was.

Everything is what it is. And nothing more—unless
our thoughts begin to distort it.

So that's what we're trying to achieve through these
Explorations: finding an overall personal context in which
we can see accurately what we experience and think. As
with the spider in the darkness, we need to protect ourselves largely when we don't see the whole picture.
We need to protect our shaky self-images only when
they are isolated and split off from our whole functioning selves. The soul is wholeness, the *all* of us.

HIDDEN IMAGES

Now, what about self-images of which we are not at all
aware? Or: what happens when I carry around a self-image
that is often so painful to me, so unacceptable to me, that
I have practically driven it out of my awareness completely,
tried to disown it, deny that it exists within me?

Is it even possible that we do this? Possible that we
can be so unaware? It *is* possible. In fact we operate from
this unawareness very often, and it is a major factor in our
souls being hidden from us under a pile of what I can only
call emotional rubbish.

These hidden negative self-images account for a lot
of the strong feeling that seems to burst through our otherwise "calm" behavior—later making us feel bad about
ourselves, yet without being able to get a handle on it. We
usually account for it, try to settle down, by using the old
criterion of "objectivity."

What I mean is this: I am talking to someone, and

suddenly he or she tells me that they have reduced their employees' Christmas bonuses by pleading a bad business year, when in fact the year was as good as the last. Sympathetic, perhaps even worried about implications for the future in terms of job security, the employees accepted the reduction without comment.

I go out the roof with anger. Instead of simply being aware that I am talking to an unpleasant, manipulative liar, I literally go out the roof and even think of smacking this person in the head. My gorge is so high, I have to get away before I blow up in pieces.

This person has hit a powerful chord inside me. What is my hidden, unacceptable image here? Have I identified with one of his workers and feel ripped off? Could be—and that sense would contribute to my self-awareness. But why the *intense* anger? More likely, and more hidden, is a sense that on some level, I—like this manipulative person—think or sense myself as cut from the same cloth. *I* am a liar, *I* am a manipulator, *I* move others, who depend on my word, around on an emotional board like chess pieces. And I hate myself for this tendency; and I carefully hide it, bury it. But when I see it in others it reminds me of this trait in myself and I blow up.

In short, I hate, I cannot stand, in others what I hate and hide within myself—what I hide from other people *and* try to hide from myself.

Instead of fixing this up inside myself, I put it out there into the other person and hate it "objectively."

Or I am listening to a woman who lets it loudly be known that she refused to marry her current husband unless he insured himself for at least $100,000. Again, I blow up—because I see women as crafty, cold leeches, and may suddenly feel that I have been taken advantage of by *my* wife. But what is really happening is that I am enraged by getting dimly in touch with *my* greed, coldness, passivity, and dependence which I see being played out unconcernedly by this woman in her own life.

In any of these instances, I can avoid awareness by simply indicting these people as "bad," "vicious," or "poisonous"—*objectively so*. And that will settle the matter and keep me out of touch with myself—until the next situation, when it will all be repeated. Again and again.

So:

EXPLORATION: This is a truly powerful one because it gets at the deeply hidden, deeply protected, self-images.

Make a three-column list, like so:

Strong Negative Feeling	*What Triggers It In The Behavior/ Words Of Others?*	*What Self-Image Am I Hiding?*

Then simply follow through. But don't stop with the list, don't just leave it on the paper. See how it works the next time you feel overly angry or overly depressed in a social encounter. *See, feel,* the buried image inside of you being triggered off by the "ugly" behavior of another person.

Here I am asking us to get involved very deeply with ourselves and to face some unpleasant aspects of our lives. We could of course forget the whole thing—but that would keep us traveling in circles, behaving like robots, or even withdrawing or running away from others. Then we would never experience the richness beneath the blocks of our long years of conditioning—the conditioning that has caused us both to think so negatively of ourselves and that at the same time has taught us not to examine our lives and become free individuals.

And what we might be coming to learn from our explorations is not just a means of expanding self-awareness in isolated areas—but a growing knowledge that an increase in individual freedom is a way of connecting with our own souls as well as with the souls of others.

If we can get even part of the way there, our lives will be radically different. We will have gotten out of our own way. And our possibilities will be solidly inside us where they belong.

8
Compassion
for Ourselves

If you've stayed with our Explorations, really done them, you've probably come up with a lot of what might seem like negative "material." Simply put, at this point you may have discovered many aspects or facets of yourself that you don't like, maybe even hate—forgetting for a moment the good, sound qualities in yourself that provide balance, that provide the context that give courage to go on exploring, to gently peel away the protective layers surrounding and hiding the soul. You might even be slightly depressed, might want to stop right here and run away instead of experiencing the feeling in order really to give it up.

But why? Why see yourself negatively? Why does viewing ourselves in a bad light seem so easy to do? Almost as if it is *natural* to do so. Why does the "bad" seem to outweigh the "good" in us—and often so powerfully?

In psychotherapy, for example, insights offered to clients are very frequently taken as attacks and humiliations rather than ways to knowledge and understanding about oneself. A therapist might tell a client that he or she has trouble connecting with other people because he comes on too strong, too aggressively, as if he "knows" everything— and people simply flee his onslaught. Too often the client takes this type of comment not as an observation but as a character assassination: his whole being, his whole self, is "seen" as fake, as no good. His secret, hidden negative self-image gets stoked up and it overwhelms him. Which is why therapists try to balance the comment with such statements as: "There's a *part* of you that needs to come on strong with others. . . . etc." But all this does is make the person feel split in pieces, more fragmented. He often becomes engaged in a war between or among his "pieces" and "parts."

You obviously don't have to peek through the keyhole of a therapy session to see this kind of thing at work. It happens to you, to all of us, almost every day. Somebody is always telling us something about ourselves that upsets us, shakes us up, makes us angry, anxious, or depressed. We generally experience this as an attack by a hostile person, and if it happens with someone we've liked or trusted, the pain is doubly intense because the "attack" seems so unexpected—a betrayal. Rarely, only in moments of great openness, do we say: "You're right! That's it!" But usually we cop out and try to dismiss the whole affair by labeling the other person "hostile" or "vicious"—even if we've asked the other person for advice.

And we've lost a moment, a precious moment, of possible self-awareness.

There's an old German proverb: if you really want to find out about yourself, ask your neighbor.

EXPLORATION: This is a little similar to the "Bowing-

Out-of-the-Argument" Exploration, but runs much deeper. The very next time you find yourself in a situation where someone is telling you something about yourself that you find uncomfortable, *just listen.* Don't defend yourself. *Remember that there is nothing to defend against except an unreal self-image built by thoughts and concepts.* Whether this person is kind or hostile is of no importance. Hear what's being said about you; see it; look at it. The other person is not an authority figure you have to be afraid of; his insight into you gives him no special power. He is just seeing something that you *do,* some way you *are,* something you've been unaware of playing out. Truth will be there, even if a lot of his own distortions enter the picture.

Even if he begins to interpret your behavior or your way of being, just listen. You have nothing to lose and a lot to gain.

Like as not, you are at first going to hate this Exploration. You might feel like a punch-drunk boxer being worked over by Muhammad Ali in his prime. You might feel enraged. Okay, breathe deeply if you have to. Don't counterpunch; don't turn the other cheek either. Just let yourself hear, let the other person—for once—finish what he has to say. Then let it be over, let there be an end to it, let it go.

The first few times you allow yourself to do this, you might well feel like a child who has been criticized or dressed down by a parent or a teacher. Actually, you *will* feel this way if you let yourself make the connection between your adult self and the timid, helpless kid who is still inside you.

Good!

You will get a clear understanding that the self-image

just under attack is one that has been formed very early in life and still hangs on to make you feel like a child—even in middle life.

You will also get a handle on a larger principle that we've been building up to: *All negative self-images, and many superficial positive images, are childish.* Not *childlike,* but completely child*ish.* And they are always preventing us from moving, growing, and discovering our souls because, being childish, they keep us stuck, trapped, pinned like flightless butterflies in a specimen case.

This is a powerful Exploration in finally learning to have compassion for ourselves—and, ultimately, compassion for others. And I mean *compassion,* not self-justification or some glib or shallow "I'm okay" statement that has no depth to it.

I mean compassion of the deepest kind, a profound soul-connection, a real self-acceptance never to be shaken again.

Because for perhaps the first time you will begin to understand that you are *not* a weak, helpless, dependent child being punished or tongue-lashed by an adult. Unlike the child, you will have *willingly* lent yourself to the encounter, entered it as an adult in the spirit of risk, adventure, and quest for self-knowledge—all those things that a child just cannot do. A child may dream of climbing Mount Everest, but he just can't do it until he grows up.

And you can look at that child still inside yourself with the compassion of your own maturity. And give it understanding, love, and acceptance; then strengthened, listened to, taken seriously, it can grow up to meet you in your grownup space and time—*now.* The fragmentation will be gone.

Self-pity is when you feel sorry for yourself, when you can't see the child, when you confuse it with your whole being.

In compassion there is not a shred of self-pity.

Compassion is all soul.

THE NEGATIVE-POSITIVE SPLIT

So then why does it seem so natural to see ourselves in a harsh, self-condemning way? Why are we so devoid of self-compassion?

It's a complicated business when you try to answer the question by looking into individual after individual. But there's a general idea that I find extremely potent, based on how we are all brought up along broader lines—early patterns that later in life we have to work so hard to reverse or undo.

To begin with, except in very rare instances, we are never taught as children to be good to ourselves, to do for ourselves, to see ourselves in a wholesome, good light *simply because we exist*. Yet that's the only reason we should see ourselves favorably—*simply because we're alive*. We owe nothing to anyone: just *being* should be good enough.

Except that it never seems to be.

We are brought up with the urgency that we have to *prove* that we're worthwhile, usually by doing, then by being, what other people want. Those others are of course our parents, but they are also engaged in doing and being what others, what the whole society, wants *them* to do and be.

So we can get here a very clear understanding of why breaking out of this ongoing circle can be accomplished *only* by individual effort, by a person, not by a group. Because the social group is the source of the pressure, and the more people you have in a group, the greater the pull toward conformity.

Now in the course of being brought up to be as our overseers want us to be, a great deal of clout is also given to the idea of helping others. For example, we still have thriving church groups, parochial schools, Sunday schools, Girl- and Boy-Scout Chapters—*ad infinitum*. These groups are efforts to get young people involved in upholding and perpetuating social values, which is obviously necessary if any society is to function without being split apart.

But it is right at this point that the split being fought against becomes so obvious in the individual.

Because side-by-side with the work for social unity comes the intense emphasis on the youngster's "need" to compete—in school, in athletics, etc. The win-lose ethic is implanted: the Little League baseball team is supposed to be a team, but the weaker players sit on the bench because the won-and-lost record inflames the adult coaches. Little boys cry when they strike out or drop a fly ball. And on and on. Competitive examinations, dogfights to enter a "good" college—and the finale of the individually competitive job market where you put out steadily or the guy behind you will walk over your dead body.

So the ostensibly "sane" schizophrenia of our bringing up has much to do with an early emphasis on doing and being for others—and then a plunge into "individuality," the survival-life of the world.

Nowhere are we urged to be good to ourselves, to be compassionate with ourselves, *really* to become individuals. We are kept dependent: dependent on parents, then on jobs, and the early training to do for others can be seen for what it is, the involvement in a life geared to security, to

"I'll scratch your back if you'll scratch mine," "I don't like him, but it's bad politics not to invite him to the party," "They *owe* us an invitation to dinner"—and all the rest of it.

There is not a bit of compassion in any of this bringing-up process because the individual person is never taught to be compassionate with himself or herself.

We are always engaged in a tightrope walk between trying to seem grown up and wanting to have our helpless inner child respected and satisfied.

So that's why we always feel so prone to attack—because we strive so desperately to maintain the self-images that hide the inner belief that we are still dependent children. The weak, helpless kid always lurking beneath the mask of independence and social prestige. We cannot accept ourselves fully unless we admit that the kid is there—and come to give it what it needs and never had: compassion.

EXPLORATION: Write this one out, using all the imagination and sensitivity you can muster up.

List *all* your childish traits—all the ones you can think of, that you're aware of. You know what many of them are.

Now write a story or an essay, or a combination of both—whatever is most natural to you—about the *child* who has these traits. *Not what the child becomes or grows up to be.* Just paint the best possible word-picture about what that *child* is like. *See* the child. *Feel* the child. Take a long time, as much time as you need.

It's a kid, *just* a kid. Only that. No more and no less.

Say hello to yourself for the first time in years.

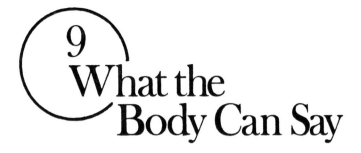

9
What the
Body Can Say

By now it should be rather clear that rediscovering the energy of the soul involves getting our fragments together, welding ourselves into the whole people we were meant to be. And we do this by seeing, examining the splits within us, then trying to smooth out the scar tissue.

So that our search for the soul is nothing less than a process of self-healing, using information that is readily available to us—information that lies within us, not theories or ideas fed to us from some outside source or "authority." Actually, most of our original difficulties, our splits, have been created by the rules and pressures of outside forces and self-styled authorities. That's why we so often find ourselves resisting advice—resisting being *told* what to do "for our own good."

There can be a very healthy suspiciousness in this position: we are reminded of the person who, anxiously complaining to his clergyman that he has lost his faith, is told to pray for its return. Which is exactly what he can't do with any conviction since his experience is that he has lost his faith and therefore his capacity to believe in the power of prayer.

We are always better off relying on the information we already have deeply within us. We are our own best feedback systems. What we *know* is *ours*. And what we've been doing is building an armory of new ways to liberate and maximize this feedback system.

THE BODY'S KNOWLEDGE

Being *us*, our bodies have over the years stored up an awesome amount of self-knowledge of which we are often unaware. There is no real body-mind split: modern biology, psychology, psychosomatic medicine, as well as the ancient spiritual disciplines (of both West and East) have finally converged into agreement on this point. The body and mind form a single unit capable of fluid or reflexive movement. Indeed, we "work" best as people, as individuals, when this unitary flow is in operation. This flow is soul-action. It happens when we are really living fully in the present.

The shortcoming of many schools of psychotherapy, and of many methods of "self-help" systems, is that either the mind *or* the body is exclusively emphasized. For example, psychoanalysis stays in the realm of the mind, maintaining that all meaningful self-knowledge is ultimately intellectual. On the other hand, many exponents of the "body therapies," such as Structural Integration or "rolfing" (a kind of deep and often painful "massage" of almost the entire surface of the body) neglect the mind. Thus any of these methods are unbalanced in one direction or another and, unfortunately, perpetuate our deep-seated thought that the body and mind are separate "things," even separate functions. Nevertheless, there is always the hope that a therapeutic approach through the intellect will help the body—and vice versa. But too frequently the hope remains just that—a hope.

There are also a small number of therapists who use both approaches in their work with a single client, either doing the whole job themselves or sharing the work with another therapist.

It can work this way:

George, a client of mine, a middle-aged professional man, had been stricken with a relatively mild case of polio as a boy. He had been a tremendous baseball player then, and had dreamed of becoming a major leaguer. The polio knocked him flat, broke his dream, shattered him, and left him with a life-long limp. And, very important, in order to protect himself from his incredible emotional pain, he blocked out, actually "forgot," almost five years of his life —the five most painful years of his life. George had no memories of this time, beginning when he first fell sick; he could only speculate, with such comments as "I must have wanted to die," "I probably wanted to give up," "All I can say is it must have been horrible." He was completely out of touch: there was not even an intellectual recollection at play.

But while the memory was split off, the body had forgotten nothing. The "split" had been self-imposed— something we do to ourselves constantly. Yet we can never get rid of the pain: *we can only pretend to by taking advantage of the body vs. mind tradition in which we've been raised*. So really he had "forgotten" nothing at all. It just seemed that way because the mind couldn't decipher the body's messages—and that's why we could no longer work meaningfully in a verbal setting with those "lost" five years.

We searched for a way to heal the artificial split, a way that he could use to inform himself, to retrieve what belonged to him.

We hit on "rolfing"—one of those apparent coincidences: he had read an article in a popular magazine while I had been recently talking to a colleague who had become interested in body work.

Within four rolfing sessions George was literally racing across town from his rolfer to my office, bursting with emotions and memories released from the storehouse of his body.

I had never experienced anything like it.

Suddenly he had to use the couch in my offce because a chair was too confining: he thrashed, kicked, flailed his arms, cried, shouted, sweated. Memories there were, plenty of them—but they were all pure emotion at the same time.

All the missing years returned, and with them all the pain. And not just the suffering or the broken dreams. He could also remember the people who helped him, who cared for him—especially his father, whose tenderness and love during that desperate time he had utterly lost touch with.

The split eventually healed.

He used his own inner information to heal himself.

I almost forgot something. We were both so involved with the excitement of what was happening that only months later did we realize an astounding change: George no longer limped.

Neither the body nor the intellectual insight erased the limp. The limp was erased by *all* of him.

And there was nothing miraculous about it.

His power, his full inner connection, his consciousness, restored the energy to his leg.

A NEW USE OF THE BODY

George underlines the power available in all of us when we heal the artificial splits we create between mind and body, soul and intellect, life without and life within.

Now, it's important to stress what most of us do with our bodies. Mainly, we either *observe* them or are unaware of them. We drape clothes on them, use them for sex, feel hunger pangs, whatever. Sometimes we even admire them. More usually we admire the bodies of others far more than we admire our own.

But, aside from sexual feelings, we seem most aware of our bodies when we become sick, when we experience pain, or when we suffer from a stab of shame. And then, if we don't have some consistent, deeply neurotic idea that we are physically ugly or deformed, we can recognize something very profound.

That is, we most often regard our bodies as enemies. We imagine that they attack us with illness, sometimes with impotence; that they mirror a "depressing" aging process (and in our society it is practically a crime to become old) that is supposed to result in neglect, retirement, and an absence of attractiveness, love, and sex; that they are the fragile containers that break down and kill us.

We believe in the immortality of the mind, of thinking.

A body in pain reminds us that nothing is immortal in its exact form.

And we live every day with the unconscious belief

that we carry around our immortality—our minds—in weak shells.

We come, usually quite without awareness, to believe that our bodies *are* really our enemies. And so we are always waging an internal war, an ongoing conflict of life and death, mind against body.

Older men often court young women in order to maintain the illusion of agelessness; they die playing tennis because a downward adjustment in their game indicates an admission of aging; they work harder to show that they can "hack it" with the cream of the new graduating class. Women get their faces lifted, their breasts siliconed, or, on a less dramatic level, dye their greying hair. They will take younger lovers if they can get them, even if they are being used emotionally and financially.

The Fountain of Youth.

Those of us who are frightened of aging become little more than prey.

Again, we need to look at our dependency and our failure to develop our inner lives, our souls, in order to understand this sad affair.

Just as we can place all our hopes for fulfillment and happiness on outside sources, so too can we treat our bodies as "things" outside the life of our hopes and desires. The body becomes something "out there"—and when it wrinkles, creaks, sags, hurts, or breaks down, it is very much like some other person who won't give us what we need, some other person who betrays us.

And it is an almost classic fact that the less we are aware of our inner life, our true meaning—the more unconscious we are—the more the body is seen as the enemy, and the sicker we become physically.

A backbone of psychosomatic medicine can be translated into a simple statement: our unawareness of ourselves erupts into physical illness.

To be aware of ourselves, to be deeply aware, to make the soul-connection, is to rid ourselves of a host of illnesses, emotional and physical.

And, needless to say, the way we regard (or don't regard) our bodies is powerfully tied into our self-images and into the state of our self-esteem. Both *must* be tattered, even to some extent demolished, if we bring our negative thoughts and judgments to bear on our bodies. Because, of course, *our bodies are us.*

We can't *feel* well about ourselves if we select one aspect of ourselves to condemn, criticize, or disregard—whether we hate the body and love the mind, or the other way around. We feel well of ourselves, we *know* we have worth, we know we have soul, only when we regard our whole being as valuable and meaningful.

To get to this point we have a whole lot of personal and collective history to get through. A thick, dense, thorny maze of it. Most of our parents have, with some degree of queasiness, been upset by our early explorations of our bodies. The religious ideal, no matter what faith is practiced, has emphasized mind and "spirit" at the expense of the body—thus, I'm afraid, not really getting at the true balance implied by the soul. Most mystic movements of the East, so attractive to modern-day Americans, definitely de-emphasize the worth of the body, at least sexually. And so it has gone, and so it goes.

What *do* we feel about our bodies? For our purposes right now, what do we *think* about our bodies, what judgments do we make that we may not be fully in touch with?

EXPLORATION: Stand naked before a mirror—if possible, a full-length mirror. Don't move; set yourself. Let your eyes contact your feet and, very slowly, move your eyes up your body. Take in, absorb, the details. *See* yourself. End by looking at your hair, then meet your eyes. Hold the gaze for a moment. But don't move your body.

First, sense how you feel inside, your emotional state. Are there any "funny" sensations? Then locate the area in which the feelings are taking place: throat, stomach, chest, genitals, whatever. Can you label the feelings? If not, fine; just let it be, you're feeling "something."

Now interpret the expression on your face. What feeling, attitude, are you giving off?

Finally, keep your eyes "flexible" (ready to look at any part of your body) while sensing and feeling where the muscular *tensions,* the stiffness and rigidity, are: stomach, thighs, the whole body? Look at these areas, then deliberately relax them. Take a deep breath if it will help.

You will probably have been aware of *some* unpleasantness. *Some* degree of tightness. Any tightness you feel is a clue to some out-of-touchness with your body.

Now get warm and sit down with a pencil and paper.

EXPLORATION: Without thinking too much, make a list of all your body parts *as you recollect them from the Exploration at the mirror. Be quick.* Avoid some subtle process that may say: "People have toes, so I must have toes," etc. Just quickly list the parts of your body. Finish. Don't revise the list.

Now return to the mirror.

Check your body against your list.

What parts did you omit?

These are the ones with which you may be least comfortable, from which you are most split off. The parts you may actually dislike, even hate. It can actually be *that* intensely negative.

There is a slight possibility that someone may not omit body parts from the list, but this is very doubtful. In any case, list the omitted parts—or, if you think you've caught them all, note the ones you like least. Then note the ones you like best. Make two columns.

If it pleases you, you can mull it all over for a little while, just noting that there are parts of your body you like, parts you dislike. Note, too, the distinct possibility that you somehow hide the parts you dislike, keep them out of awareness, even wish they didn't exist. If you want, you can construct reasons for the likes and dislikes. For a moment it doesn't matter what they might be.

Remember Mark? In doing this Exploration he discovered something that at first glance seemed entirely playful, entirely whimsical. He gave identities to two parts—the surface of his abdomen and his right hand. Kiddingly—at first—he described the surface of his stomach as a man of leisure who did no work, basked in the sun, could run to fat, was carried around passively. Personified, this "man" was a country gentleman who wore tweeds and ascots, drank fine wines and brandies, smoked the best cigars, kept horses and hounds, had a magnificent library, and wintered in St. Tropez.

Mark's hand, however, was a hard worker who rested only during sleep, almost a complete drudge, always tired, and drastically underpaid. Personified, he was tough and lean, physical, with crewcut hair. He wore jeans and a teeshirt, drank beer, read Mickey Spillane and James Bond.

Suddenly, what had begun as a lark became serious business (remember the power of playfulness). One of the large, extremely large, splits in Mark's personality became clear to him. These two radically opposed images lived within him—the leisurely gentleman and the exhausted laborer, the rich man and the poor man, the upper class and the lower, the *intellectual* and the *physical.*

He became aware of an incredible conflict within: if too "successful," the poor man tried to pull him down; if he acted too "lower class," too informal, too spontaneous, the intellectual formal man scorned him. He saw that he was caught in an emotional no-man's land—and would always be caught until the two "men," the two aspects of himself could freely unite and merge into a whole person, a whole identity, each contributing what the other lacked. A *real* self-image.

The details of the "why" of Mark's conflict, the causes of the split, are not terribly important here, but it had to do with a war between wanting to be like his working-man father and the "fine" man his mother urged him to become.

Intellectually, Mark had understood a lot of this, but he had never *seen* it, never had the images, a way to enter the conflict with feeling and *experience.*

His *own* body opened it all up for him. As well as his sense of play.

DIALOGUES WITH THE BODY

So here, reflected by Mark's dialogue between two parts of his body, we have another key to understanding, and a new way of getting into, the conflict raging in our split-off self-images. Except that now we go to a level deeper than in our construction of lists—from a point farther outside to a point nearer the core of ourselves. Nearer the core because the body, as we've already indicated, is a truer, more emotional place than our mind of thoughts. It's a storehouse of our images, a permanent record of them, and not a kind of shifting "movie" produced by the endless stream of our thoughts.

The body is solid; it molds itself to our feelings about ourselves. Solid but plastic: for instance, if we are afraid of others because we think we are insecure, then we might tighten up our shoulders, "scrunch," and the mark of our insecurity is right there, visible and sometimes even physically felt, in the distortion of our postures. (Mark's identification with his working-man father was partly "locked" in his hands—as you might expect.)

And so much of what and how we think of ourselves governs the ways in which we unconsciously put forth or expose or hide the parts of our bodies that we don't like, that give us "trouble." This can be most obvious in what we do with our genitals. Women and men can avoid any kind of sexual contact: more, women might not have orgasms or might experience them only occasionally; men can go the route of full or sporadic impotence. In any of these cases, there may well be, probably *is,* some hidden self-image working against full sexual comfort and self-acceptance.

We can discover what this is and work out of it—and always increasingly gather together the loose strings of our self-connectedness.

The body can be permeated with locked-in soul. The release of it is another step toward unified reflexive action. Like the pianist who never dwells on the movements of her fingers, or the hockey player who can't even "remember" the direction he took in scoring at the net. There is no difference, no split, between head, hands, and keys; between player, stick, puck, and goal. *It's all one flow.*

In the strongest moments of life, everything is united. *The power of the movement is produced by soul.* We've *all* had moments like this. We can recollect the setting, the events—but we can't recapture the *experiences*. We can only have them again. And that's the goal (if we *must* look at things in terms of goals, which is *so much* our way of looking at things). To get such moments closer and closer together in time.

And we need the body to help us.

EXPLORATION: Choose a part of your body you like, and one that you don't like. Hold a dialogue between them. Give them each a full identity: names, occupations, whole "life-styles." Don't write anything down unless you really want to; you can just act out the play.

You'll soon see the conflict emerge, the split, the parts of your body that you've symbolized as the different negative and positive images of your entire self. Or *selves,* as it often turns out to be.

Take the drama as far as you wish—the further and deeper the better. Let the dialogue, the feelings, roll: the anger, hurt, disappointments, accusations. Let it all out. And soon the war will end and you will have further welded the splits.

I have never met anyone who failed to *see* as a result of this Exploration.

There are many further Explorations you can make following this basic one:

1. Dialogues between only those body parts you like;
2. Between those body parts you dislike;
3. Between the liked parts and "all" of you;
4. Between "all" of you and the disliked parts;
5. Between those parts you merely see as "different" from each other.

Who, in all these Explorations, is the critic? The approver? Do you truly *feel, sense,* that either or both is *you*?

Yourself? Or can you hear some voice from the past telling you what to be, how to be, what is good or bad about you? Stay with this if you can.

The power gathered in really *seeing* these opposing, conflictual self-images as they work in both the mind and body, is immeasurable. And seeing in this way is the most important aspect of what we are doing. The rest of the journey begins to follow by itself.

THE UNSEEN BODY

There is an entire surface of the body that we can justifiably call "unseen"—except for occasional and usually unplanned glimpses, and always when mirrors are accidentally positioned at unexpected angles.

Our backs and buttocks.

The implications of these "unseen" parts are enormous. Not being able easily to look at them, they are strangers to us, aliens. And we generally find strangers and aliens at least mysterious, at worst enemies against whom we have constructed well-developed prejudices.

"Low-back pain," one of the commonest and most nagging ailments in our culture, is located in an unseen area. (Indeed, so is all back pain.) Doctors rarely get a diagnostic bead on it. It just doesn't seem to make sense in our complex of physical illnesses—despite your feeling it as such. You frequently are sent to a psychotherapist. Or you get Valium.

I have personally administered psychological tests to dozens of people with this complaint, because the medical computer rarely has anything to print out. These folks usually don't like their work, or work too much; and they both blame the work for "crippling" them and then use the complaint to stay home from work. The same pattern holds true in the setting of any obligation thought of as an unwanted, but necessary-to-perform, responsibility. So the circle is a vicious one.

But the main thing, so far as I'm concerned, is that such people feel terribly *persecuted* by their backs. They feel not only attacked by them, but held back, brutally restrained by them.

Emotionally, they move ahead *very slowly, very carefully*. Taking risks is almost totally out of the question. They feel blocked from forward inner movement by something holding them back—and, pun intended, *holding their backs*. They have an extremely difficult time looking inside themselves: because this looking represents forward emotional movement.

As for the buttocks: not only are they unseen, they have a host of unpleasant psychological facts and fantasies attached to them, often around bowel functions, passing air, etc. As a rolfer friend of mine puts it: "Almost everybody gets upset when we work on the buttocks. It's not that everybody is 'tight-assed' in the emotional, uptight sense. Everybody seems 'tight-assed' in actual physical terms."

What we don't know—more, what we can't *see*, is a source of trouble for us.

Physical attack is almost always conceptualized as coming from the rear, from behind us. And yet it doesn't, at all, always happen this way; in fact it rarely does.

And emotional "attack" is similarly conceived as emerging from something we can't see. That is, from out of our unawareness. We feel "stabbed in the back" by Pearl Harbor, by an untrustworthy acquaintance, by a mugger, by physical pain, by an attack of anxiety or depression, by many of our dreams.

We keep our backside, all of it, tensed against some sort of attack (the vast majority of us have extremely poor posture, which you can largely trace to a distortion of the back) in the same way that we keep our soul hidden from ourselves. The fear of the unexpected, or what we can't *see*.

EXPLORATION: Do the mirror trick. Examine your en tire back from the bottom up, in the same way you examined your front. Hold the dialogues after seeing what you like, dislike, are neutral toward. Hold dialogues between parts of the back and parts of the front.

Get used to it.

What you *can* see can't hurt you.

THE HIDDEN BODY

Now it's very possible that there are things about the *inner* body that you dislike or are plain afraid of. No one seems to *like* his or her heart, lungs, kidneys, or stomach. Again, we are aware of them almost exclusively when they hurt us or when they malfunction, or when we think of them prior to an upcoming physical exam. (We can like our teeth because they may show well in a smile, or dislike them if they show badly.) Some of us eat properly to fend off illness, but rarely in order to show respect for our insides. Consumers of organic foods are often more set on counteracting the poisonous effects of chemical additives than on superior nutrition (and along this line, established medical schools have traditionally not offered a *single* course on nutrition). The average person hasn't got the foggiest idea about what goes on inside the body.

Yet the inner body is what must function well to keep us alive.

It's all a great mystery—and it would seem that we want to keep it so.

Largely we *don't* like what's inside. As a little girl once said to me: "It's *yucky*."

Or we try to deny what's there because we've equated it only with trouble and the possibility of disease. What we don't know won't hurt us? What we don't know about ourselves is *exactly* what hurts us. And if we really cared, we would care what we put into this container holding our physical existence. Would we drink? Smoke? Eat junk food? Take drugs?

We no doubt know more about the workings of the stock market, how the New York Yankees are doing, local politics, what our neighbor's life-style is like, than we know about the functioning of our own bodies.

Plain and simple, most of us are scared to death of our physical insides—as we are also often afraid of our emotional insides.

And that is another roadblock to the discovery of the energy and freedom of the soul. Soul is the connection between in and out, physically as well as emotionally.

EXLORATION: A very simple one that will cost you a few dollars and a few hours of time.

Go to a bookstore and buy a good, illustrated, nontechnical book on the human body, both male and female. See and learn what's inside, how it all works.

And be aware of your feelings as you read the text and study the pictures. Get the knowledge, the "objective" data; but also get in touch with the emotional charge involved. Let yourself feel: there's quite an impact in confronting your heart, your brain; quite an impact in truly believing that you have all this vital stuff packed inside a few square feet of skin.

Come to see your body as something that makes you physically alive, keeps you alive. Not as something that can attack you, kill you, at the drop of a hat.

Conceive of the soul in the same way.

EXPLORATION: By this time you should be pretty adept at holding dialogues with parts of your external body. Now begin to hold them with the internal parts—the ones you like, dislike, are mystified by, whatever. The parts you dislike will probably be those that seem to give you trouble: the stomach that gets sick or sour; the head that aches (headaches are obviously internal, though the outer skin gets sensitive and hurts as well); the eyes that have ceased to be clear-sighted; the lungs that feel pressured after exercise or climbing stairs.

Liking is more difficult. You might not "like" anything inside—but that's mostly a function of being split off from, and not being familiar with, what's there. So get to know these parts, talk to them. Again, they keep you alive—and they help you *enjoy* living. They *are* you. Not just a piece of you.

If we can be nice to other people because we hope they will make us feel good, we can become friendly with our insides for the same reason. And I can't stress this enough: our insides keep us *alive,* not just make us feel good.

Hold all sorts of dialogues, in the same patterns as with the external parts. What you will begin to know about yourself is beyond calculation, beyond even words.

Finally, what you might also try is to understand the relationship between your external body and your inner organs, and unfortunately this is easiest when something inside hurts. For example, when we are cut down by a severe headache we tend to place our hands on the painful places, even lightly massage them with our fingertips. Get at the relationship, the ongoing dialogue, between head and hand. See what they are saying to each other. what the head wants from the hand, what the hand is trying to do. And if *this* is the case, learn why the hand can't help the head, perhaps even why the head won't let it.

You might begin to learn why, in the broader scope of life, you have trouble letting all of you be of greater help to yourself.

The key to getting what you want, to living a soul-connected life, is not reliance on good advice or following some well-traveled road. The key is the discovery of what you are putting in your own way. Then removing it.

The dialogues will help open you to this self-knowledge.

They are crucial tools even in telling you *why* you might be physically ill. The body, in sickness, is giving you a powerful message.

See sickness as a message.

Accept it as a message to your whole being, to your whole way of living.

See and accept all of it in this spirit—from a sprained ankle to a heart attack. See what your body is trying to tell you about the way *all* of you lives.

Remember my client who almost died after his heart attack? He picked up the message loud and clear, and set about changing his life. (At one point, he even said: "I never lived until I got sick.") If he hadn't, if he had denied the significance of it all, if he had chalked it off to a "bad" heart, period, he would, quite simply, have died.

He understood what had happened to him right at the core of understanding:

You don't get a heart attack (or tension headaches or, for that matter, almost anything else) simply from "bad genes" or the pressures of daily survival.

It happens because we too often live at an external pace completely out of step with our own natural inner pace. We live against nature, against the natural flow of life. And when we do that we must get sick, physically, emotionally, or both. Obviously, we can even die from this forced march through life.

EXPLORATION: The next time you plan to get sick— and what I mean by "plan" is when you are ready to get drunk (when you are aware that you get hung over), or smoke grass (which might give you headaches), or eat something that you know usually backfires on you, or dress poorly in bad weather—the next time you plan to get sick, have a dialogue between the "you" who is ready to do this and the part of you that is going to suffer.

Hold this dialogue along the lines of a conversation between you and your closest, most needed and loved, friend, who perceives that you are on the brink of hurting him or her. See this friend as a person who is not accusing you of a deliberate effort to be hurtful, but who is suggesting to you that you are going to be hurtful *because you are unaware.* See this friend (and that's what any of your body organs is) as telling you that you have hurt him many times in the past—and that while he realizes that the hurt comes from your lack of awareness, it *nevertheless* hurts him. And eventually, if you don't begin to see this, he'll have to quit the relationship. Powerless himself, he has no choice but to leave it up to you.

That's how our hearts quit on us. And our livers, stomachs, all of it.

That's how *all* our friends quit on us.

And how we quit on ourselves.

Through our lack of awareness. Our lack of soul.

EXPLORATION: If and when you *do* get sick, dialogue with all of you and your sick part. The sick part can be a one-shot stomach ache or even a "condition"—a case of migraine headaches, a lingering "bad back." Like as not, medications haven't helped you the way you've wanted them to; maybe the dialogues will shed some light.

Don't blame the part, don't blame yourself in the usual way we do this—via remorse, calling ourselves stupid, etc.

Let the sick part talk to you. And listen. The sick part won't "blame" you. Only your thoughts will, and they don't belong in this dialogue.

Like the friend, just be aware of what he or she is saying to you. Listen and get the message of the small truthful voice inside you.

Listen to it.

And connect with it.

Finally, get at the heart of what happens the next time you cancel a date or stay home from work by "playing sick." This is the first excuse that occurs to all of us when we wish to avoid an important encounter or when we wish to do "something else."

Most everyone accepts this excuse, don't they? Not only accepts it, but *uses* it as well.

Could it be, could it *really* be, that we need at least the *idea* of sickness in our society to mask our secret desires and actions?

And therefore to remain dependent because we don't say and do what we wish?

To be sick *is* to be dependent. The idea of sickness is a dependent idea. And we are subtle enough in our era of psychologizing to know that the idea can flow into physical fact.

Do we really *need* sickness?

A fascinating question. And a frightening one.

Only *you* can say.

10
The Inner Vision

We all have fantasies. Fantasies of power, sex, revenge—and you can identify a vast number of others from personal experience.

Psychotherapists will often ask their clients:

"What's your fantasy about that?" Or: "Did you have any fantasies while that was happening?" There are endless variations on the theme.

I suspect the question is, more often than not, relatively pointless—and definitely misleading. Because it's usually based on an assumption that fantasy is somehow "different" from thinking—or that fantasy is a kind of *high-powered* thought, *yet* different, perhaps more vivid, more "imaginative."

But it's not different at all.

It has nothing to do with imagination, a process which is rooted in inner creativity. And creativity has almost nothing to do with fantasy.

Like thinking used in the wrong place, fantasy is unspontaneous and stereotyped. It moves us away from ourselves and it's repetitive, stale. It has the same purpose always, it's a constant: remember my client who had the "fantasy" (but really an obsessive thought) that he would "zonk" his competitors by driving an expensive car through their neighborhoods?

So that the fantasy-thought can serve to fulfill some kind of wish or need—usually one that we can't pull off in the everyday world.

In this case the "fantasy" is an escape. More powerful than daydreaming about winning a lottery or lying on a tropical beach sipping Piña Coladas with a beautiful man or woman—but an escape nevertheless.

EXPLORATION: Back to the pencil and paper. Make a list of some of your fantasies. Just jot them down, even using a few key words, a shorthand, to keep them in mind. Then put them in categories, label them: again, sex? power? money?

A number of facts should become obvious. First, you will recognize many of these fantasies as old companions, old acquaintances. They've been with you for a long time, and their form, their content, their direction, will be basically the same today as they were yesterday.

See what I mean by stereotyped, stale?

This underlines the point I tried to make about thinking: the thoughts, the "fantasies," were with you in the past and they deal with something you would like to happen now. But nothing is happening now except the act of having the fantasy. And when it's over, there's *still* nothing. And if your fantasies are pointed toward the future, you can see even more clearly that the past and the future are tied together, *are really identical*, while the *now* is lost.

Fantasy obliterates the now. So fantasy is an escape.

The second piece of crucial information in this Exploration is learning, seeing, the major areas of your frustration and feelings of unfulfillment.

All you have to do is tote up the number of categories in which you've placed your fantasies. That is, discover if most of your fantasies fall into the areas of money, sex, power, whatever. And then you might ask yourself why you're stuck there, why you don't make it better. You might be playing the old "If . . . Then" game. So you see that the thought, "*If* I ask my boss for a raise, *then* he will fire me," is absolutely no different from what we call a "fanstasy."

So fantasies can either be positive or negative: the tropical beach or the unemployment line. Exactly the same as thoughts.

The misunderstanding here, the frequent failure to see this sameness of thought and fantasy, seems to stem from the idea that fantasies are more vibrant, more secret, deeper, even more "visual" than thoughts. Somehow more important. But they aren't at all: at best it's like putting an extra sweater on a child when the weather isn't really that cold. She doesn't need it, but to the observer the outfit *seems* a bit more complete—no matter that the child is weighed down for no sensible or true reason.

Fantasies, like the chatter of useless thoughts, are nothing but burdens that mask the possibilities of truth.

Not only that, they are just as compulsive as anything else we *have* to do. Because we rarely, if ever, sit down in order deliberately, with purpose, to "have" a fantasy. They seem to descend upon us, as if from somewhere outside us, like the endless chain of thoughts that might keep us awake half the night. That's why somebody invented the term *day-*

dream. We find ourselves staring out the window or just into space; we jump if someone interrupts us; we might ruin whatever we've been working on. We've had no awareness of our drift away; we've been "captured."

Daydream: lost in thought. Not much difference at all.

Let's keep this in mind, because we are going to make a great distinction between fantasy and active visualization. Their boundaries are really crystal clear.

Fantasy is compulsive, with no choice and no real activity. It's an escape from everyday situations, and an escape that has no power to change or even move anything. It destroys the now. It's old and stagnant. It tells you that you're stuck.

ACTIVE VISUALIZATION

Mark again. One of his dialogues with death in a visualization. And I can't demonstrate more strongly the difference between fantasy and an active use of the imagination—the creative imagination that is such a powerful tool in contacting the soul and loosening the energy wasted in fantasies and circular thinking:

I want to run. God, how I want to run! I sit there and I can't move, and I watch it—this solid black thing in front of me. It's shapeless but it's moving, not moving toward me, not moving away—just moving. Pulsating. Breathing. I want to run, but I can't. No, not can't— maybe *don't want to*. I stare hard at it. I'm trying to talk.

"Go away."

"Don't worry. It's not time."

I'm sweating. I feel it running into my eyes.

"Why now? If it's not time, why now?"

"I'm always here. You're just seeing me for the first time."

"I don't want to see you."

"Then turn your back. As always, turn your back."

That makes me angry.

"What do you mean, 'As always, turn your back?'"

"You've never seen me before because you haven't wanted to."

"Why should I want to see you?"

He doesn't answer me. I'm listening now. I hear a sigh, as if he's tired. His voice is tired.

"Haven't you had enough of running away? Hasn't everybody had enough of running away?"

He sounds so resigned.

"I've been with you from the moment you were born."

"That's horrible!"

"There's nothing horrible about it. That's the way it is. You could have seen me a lot sooner. If only you'd stopped running."

"I never knew I was running from you."

"You run from yourself. I'm just here."

"But I don't want to die."

"I said it wasn't time yet."

"Then why are you here?"

"Because of you. Because you want to see me now. As I said, I'm always here, waiting to be seen if you want to see."

I feel good about that; it makes me braver and it makes me angry again.

"So you're hanging around waiting to kill somebody else?"

Just now, as soon as I said that, I felt stupid.

"I don't *kill* anybody."

"What about people who suffer from cancer? People who are sick all their lives. Little kids who never did anyone any harm?"

"That's not my business. I haven't got anything to do with that. I'm just there when I have to be."

"Somebody pulls a name out of a hat, says, 'That's it,' and you do your job."

"If that's the way you see it, then that's the way you see it. It's also not my business to explain. Even if I could."

"But what *about* those people?"

"You're running again."

"What do you mean?"

"You're hiding behind some principle. You're angry at something you can't accept. What you won't face in yourself you try to face by looking at what happens to other people."

"Maybe. It's just that I've never had any experience with death. My parents are alive; I've never even gone to a funeral."

"And what would that tell you? What would that tell you about death? The only thing you'd feel would be the loss of somebody. You'd still know nothing about it— nothing at all. Because it didn't happen to *you*."

"So how can anybody know *anything* about it?"

"Oh, there's a way. A way to understand *something* about it."

"Tell me."

He doesn't seem to want to go on with it. Wait, something's happening. The darkness; it doesn't look so terribly dense.

"Stop hanging on to things without knowing *why.* Just stop hanging on to things."

Christ! He's fading away. Paul, he's fading away and there's so much more I want to ask him.

"Let him go," I say. "You can always go back and talk to him. For the time being, why not do what he told you? Don't hang on to him."

There was, of course, no *thing* called "Death" sitting in the room with us. Like my client who finally brought himself to "leap" from the window, Mark had his eyes closed and was conducting an inner dialogue with death, but death only as *he* could grasp it: a dark mass, not quite personified, yet with an understandable voice using common words.

It was within Mark all his life: "I've been with you from the moment you were born." He had to contact death in a way he could understand, a way he could deal with. In other people, death can wear an infinite number of guises; it can even resemble the sort of "Grim Reaper" we've seen in pictures: old, bearded, carrying a scythe.

It doesn't matter what it looks like, or even whether it's a male or female. What matters in such a visualization is the willingness and desire to meet and confront it *internally,* and to let the encounter unfold and lead to meaning.

Fantasies of death, *thoughts* of death, are almost always avoided—and that's precisely what relegates them to the level of fantasy. Fear without control, anxiety, sometimes panic. Fear about the thought.

But fear ends when we go into things, when we go into the unknown in order to see what's there.

Fear ends when we enter *ourselves.*

Nothing external can save me from death. But inside I can *see* what I think I am frightened of. And also what can make me happy and connected.

Death is only one example—but a *crucial* one—of what we can contact through creative visualizing and inner action.

The possibilities are infinite.

Because the answers are within us.

SEEING CREATIVITY WITHIN

Why do we *need* to look inside in this way? Because, short of painting or composing music or writing, *using our personal imagination is the only way in which we can be truly creative.* There is *no* other way. Only by the force and power of our imaginations can we see the vast riches within in—and then use these riches to form and shape and direct our lives into one whole creative process.

We constantly refer to life itself as something that has *been* created. And religious people refer to their god as the Creator.

Why leave it there? Shouldn't we engage in a perpetual process of creating our lives over and over again?

Imagine it: our own lives as our own best creations. *Us.*

Maybe creation is the prime meaning of life. Constant reflexive creativity. Second nature.

Soul.

But how do we do it? Where do we go?

We go inside.

We can buy a palette, a spectrum of colors, and canvasses. But we can't put out anything into the world if it doesn't come from the inside.

All you really have to know about this process is that the inner life is a powerhouse, bursting with creative energy that wants very strongly to pour out and inform our lives in the day-to-day world. There's no mystery to this. It will just happen when the energy is released, because what prevents this inner-outer connection is our traditional contempt for, and fear of, the images and feelings within. We dam them up; we pretend they have little or no meaning. Or we are afraid that our daily "responsibilities" will be undermined by forces beyond our control.

What we mean, of course, is that we don't want anything "unpleasant" to pop out at us, to swamp us, to make us anxious, depressed, fearful, apathetic.

But if we fight off the unpleasant, we necessarily fight off the strength, the joy. If we dampen one emotion, we dampen them all. When we are frightened of "something" within us, we are making the flat statement that we are not in touch, are unaware, don't know ourselves.

Getting there is not an intellectual process.

Remember my client, the woman who *consciously* thought of herself as a sick woman, a hypochondriac, a person whom doctors called a "crock?" Using her creative imagination in a visualization she *understood* that she didn't see herself as sick; she could drop her self-image of a physical disaster area. A world could open: a world previously inaccessible to "sick" people.

Another client, who "felt" himself to be an empty, ugly, and destructive person, has a visualization in which his inner space is a warm, comfortable room paneled by good, solid, burnished wood, a room with soft leather-bound books and a cozy fire in the hearth. As if by magic, a woman enters, and in his imagination he allows himself to get close to her—closer and closer. And in time he allows himself to become close to a woman in the outer world; and he discovers that he is as sound, as attractive, as wholesome as the room itself. He has his first important, giving and taking realtionship.

Not *one* word passed between us. No interpretations, no leading statements, no guiding. *It just happened.* The inner vision, the inner life, flowed out: he informed himself. *He saw.*

And Mark, who was never able to communicate with his father chalked it off to the old man's passivity, weakness, and detachment:

> He's sitting on the coffee table. I mean he's *tiny,* sitting in a tiny chair in the middle of the table, the size of a doll. Five or six inches tall. And I'm huge compared to him—as big as a real person. Maybe bigger. That's *him,* all right, small, removed, not giving a damn. I need something to be able to talk to him. What? A bullhorn to make him hear me? I need *something.* Good God, I wish you could see what I'm doing! I'm putting on a helmet, a Roman gladiator's helmet. And now I have a round shield and a flat, broad, double-edged sword. Sandals and thongs around my calves. And he's still there on the table, like a toy. . . .

So he finally confronts his "weak," "passive," father—defended and armed like a warrior in Caesar's legions. Not "as if" he is a Roman legionnaire. There are no "symbols" here. He *is* a legionnaire. *That's* the strength he needs to face this "weakling" of a father.

Again, no words. No symbolic interpretations. Would any be needed?

He *saw*. And with very little effort he changed the terms of the "real" relationship. By "real" I mean the one that takes place at a physical, concrete coffee table over actual steaming coffee—but there is no way to escape the irony in the use of the word.

Inner = Outer.

And that's the best equation we can form.

THE CONTEXT

To go ahead with our visualizations, we need to give ourselves a context. Recall my client who was at first frightened of the spider looming in the darkness, then placed it in a natural setting where it became no more, no less, than what it was.

That's a bit the way we are going to establish our individual contexts, the setting of our inner worlds, our inner realities. Because without a context nothing really makes sense; without finding our inner settings, pieces and fragments hang loose in the darkness and we don't see them for what they are. We need a field, a place, a base of operations from which we can begin, wander from, enter the unknown, create, and to which we can always return. So:

EXPLORATION: Setting the place, the space within. The time of day is unimportant, but it's always best to do your visualizations when you're not tired and when your head isn't flooded by a list of things to do, chores to be accomplished.

Sit quietly and comfortably, relaxed but with good

posture, in a room as free as possible of noise or any other distractions. Close your eyes and begin to breathe deeply, evenly, calmly. (Some people doing this for the first time become a bit nervous right at this point. If you do, don't worry about it; the feeling should pass after a while.) Focus on your breathing until you feel completely relaxed. Don't "fight off" any thoughts that may emerge; don't "follow" them either. Just concentrate on your breathing—its rise and fall, inhalation and exhalation, its movement in your body.

Now visualize a door.

Don't "think" a door.

See one.

Work on the door with your imagination. Make it exactly the way you want it: large, small, plain, elaborately paneled, perhaps French doors, any color you wish. This is the door through which you will enter your place, your setting, your context.

Keep *seeing* the door, working at it, until you're completely satisfied with it, until it looks *just so*.

Then, at your own pace, your own speed, open it. If it's locked, produce a key—from your pocket, the thin air, it doesn't matter. And unlock the door.

Walk through and *see what's there*. The door can lead *into* a place or *out into* a place—a room or the outdoors.

Some people will *see* immediately. Others will have to work harder to construct the scene in their imaginations.

Remember that this is *your* scene, *your* setting, and that *you can do anything you want with it.*

Anything is possible in the inner world of the imagination.

You are going to "get around the rules" of science.

Now, whatever pops into your sight, let it happen. If it's a room, decorate it in any way you see fit; if it's some place outdoors, provide the scenery.

No hints here. This experience *must go your way,* and your way only. But don't think; or at least avoid such thoughts as: "This is a living room; it *should* have a couch." Just go ahead and do it—any way you want. You have all the materials, all the possibilities of the universe at your disposal. *You can do anything you want.*

Get *your* place. That's the basic point of this Exploration. *See* everything. Walk around. Touch things. Smell them. Stay as long as you like. Linger. Use all your senses.

When you've stayed as long as you wish, and are ready to leave, remember that you can get back to this place any time at all, whenever you want. Now don't leave abruptly, don't suddenly open your eyes. Let the scene fade, let the images pass by your senses. Become aware of your breathing again; feel your body in the chair; tune into the room noises, outside noises.

Then gently open your eyes and sit calmly for a few minutes.

As I suggested above, for a great many of us, this Exploration may not come easily. It may require work— at least in the beginning. Because in many ways it's almost like creating, forging, contacting, our own *inner reality* for the very first time in our lives. *Deliberately* making the contact. With purpose.

It's not a dream, nor is it a fantasy, nor a chain of thoughts. It's an actual connection with our inner vision and inner power—and a great step in touching the energy of our souls.

Now, in any subsequent visualization you perform, the way in remains the same. Just follow the same relaxation procedure before putting yourself where you wish to be. You can always start from your place, touching base there and then venturing out—and then returning there before coming back to the *outer* reality.

There really is no limit to what you can do in your explorations into your possibilities and meaning. You can fly, become an animal in order to see what life is like from *that* level of existence—*literally do anything.*

You might want to leave your place as a grasshopper. If so, sit on a leaf by the side of a pond. See the *largeness* of a leaf, of a drop of dew. Let yourself be the size of a grasshopper. This ability will come with time. And at first you might experience yourself as *watching* the grasshopper. With practice it shouldn't be too difficult actually to *become* the grasshopper.

I can share with you a personally fascinating experience. One of my house plants was dying, its leaves turning a crisp brown. Nothing seemed able to restore it. One night I spontaneously visualized myself as a tiny person and climbed into the pot holding the plant. Opening a door in the stem I was aware of a tremendous heat coming from the roots, as well as a fiery glow.

It turned out that the plant was being destroyed by an excess of chemical fertilizer that was literally burning away the roots.

Now before we go on, there is one point I would like to make *absolutely clear* so that these Explorations don't "degenerate" into fantasy. There is no intention here to escape from life, from boredom, or from anything else— nor to obtain some sort of relief or pleasure.

The purpose is to explore our inner lives and find, learn, see what's there—and to engage life. No matter what we come up with. So we are going to be both active and receptive—receptive to what happens, responsive to what happens. But not passively captured and worked *on* by a stereotyped thought-fantasy that sheds no light, that is simply a circular happening that leads nowhere.

So what we want to stimulate in our visualizations is an inner *spontaneity* of feeling, seeing, and action—which will lead to the same sort of spontaneity in the outer everyday world. We can't have it in the outer world if it is blocked and dammed up within us. *That is simply not possible.* And since all meaning, soul, emanates from within, the way from in to out is a logical one.

Is it conceivable that we could meet a person who is *truly* spontaneous and free and connected socially—but locked, rigid, out of touch within? It *isn't* possible. If someone comes off that way, then he or she is one hell of an actor—and one hell of a fragmented person.

This flow from in to out—that's why it begins to happen by itself after we get deeply into the visualizations. Because it *has* to happen if we begin where everything starts: inside. It has to happen because we are constantly moving inside; and while this movement can be slowed down or blocked to some greater or lesser extent, it can never be stopped. We are dead if it stops. Literally dead. And once the inner contact and awareness begin to loosen the blocks, the rubbish we heap up against the flow, the movement is liberated and the inner-outer connection begins to weld itself into a seamless golden thread.

And don't be afraid that the dam will burst and you'll be flooded. Nothing will burst if you move at your own pace and don't force or push. Unfortunately in our culture we are too often forcers and pushers—and too often we fall on our faces as a result of the useless momentum.

Take your time, find your pace, and you will move with the flow, not against it.

THE GUIDE

As your visualizations progress and deepen, a "guide" may spontaneously appear. The guide may be a person, perhaps an animal. One woman's guide is a stag; a man's is an eagle-like owl. Or you might want to create a guide or a companion to accompany you on your inner journeys. Sometimes we need a little help, a little encouragement— and we can get it directly from within. Here's an example:

> I'm standing, facing into a kind of dense milky cloud and I can't see where to go. There doesn't seem to be any way in, no path, nothing. . . . Ooh! There's this huge owl standing next to me —human-size, and he also resembles an eagle. He doesn't do or say anything, but I know I can hop on his back. So I do, and I stretch out my arms and hold on. He flies into the cloud, through it, and the whiteness is all around me. Now we're coming out of it, the clouds break, and we're flying over the ocean. My owl is much larger now and I'm lying very comfortably on his back. It's beautiful, gloriously beautiful. Flying, with this shimmering blue ocean beneath us. . . .

The owl, of course, is this man's own inner power and wisdom, which he uses to enter and penetrate whatever is being hidden from him. Once he discovered this power, it was not difficult to release it into the outer world. He could begin to penetrate the unknown, could begin to take many more chances. He simply became aware of a power within him that he had never experienced before.

And that's all there is to it.

It all happens by itself, without thinking or working—or making choices.

Why should it be any other way? How *can* it be any other way if it's *real*? And if it's *your* way, it *has* to be real.

So your guide, if you want one, or if one happens to appear, will be the best kind of guide. It won't be someone who "sees" you through the dogma of religious systems like Judaism or some forms of Christianity, or through some microsopic theory of personality like psychoanalysis. Your guide will be another newly discovered aspect of yourself. Your guide will be you.

Finally, you can do visualizations using any *external* situation you wish to penetrate, understand on a feeling and intuitive level—any situation you may want to influence or try to change. From a simple dialogue with an alienated friend, to a cosmic flight, to an encounter with death—like Mark's.

But there is yet another pool of images we can plumb in order to delve even deeper into ourselves. Images that appear spontaneously and regularly from the bottom line of consciousness. Images that tell no lies, that are bursting with pure meaning.

The images of our dreams.

11
Dreams:
The Ultimate
Adventure

There is no such thing as a bad dream.

That doesn't mean that the feelings we experience in dreams are fake, artificial, or meaningless—especially when they appear to be negative. It means that dreams are exactly what they are—*our deep messages to ourselves.* They can be startling, frightening, awesome; but the idea, the judgment, that they're "bad" is a thought that occurs after we wake up.

Thoughts again.

We tend to place value judgments on our dreams. Roughly, if something about them scares us or leaves us anxious, they become "bad" as we look back at them. If pleasant, they are "good." If puzzling, but not especially emotional, we might just shrug them off.

And many of us make the classic statement: "It's only a dream."

As if what's at the deepest levels of ourselves has no meaning.

Unfortunately, many of us might well believe that. While others become anxious when they don't intellectually understand something about themselves—so anxious that they are willing to discard the messages from the soul, to deny their meaning.

To say that my dream "is only a dream," to say that in the sense of dismissing it, is to say: "My life is only a life." Unimportant.

The danger, of course, in denying or cutting off any part of our existence, is the danger we've discussed before: our lives become fragmented, broken to pieces, disconnected.

Let's get rid of the mystique of dreams—and with the mystique the thought that they are impenetrable, dark, scary. Why shouldn't we be able to fathom ourselves at this level? What has made it so difficult for us to stir up our awareness about such a powerful force within us?

Here's part of the problem:

Much has been written about dreams. In some ways, maybe too much, because the possible clarity has become lost, swamped, in a whole lot of technical jargon aimed at psychotherapists who are placed in positions of being interpreters of dreams—and in many instances, some therapists rather inflatedly believe that they can tell a person more about his dreams than that person can tell himself.

And much of this technical approach focuses on uncovering the "true" meaning of symbols. Symbols, in fact, may be the least important aspect of dreaming. But such has been the emphasis on them, that even in modern theories they have become little or no different from to A-to-Z entries in Gypsy dream almanacs. A fortune-teller may interpret a dream snake as an omen of an impending attack, a psychoanalyst as a penis. What, really, is the difference in the approach? What, really, does it tell the dreamer about himself or herself? There is absolutely no justification for turning one thing into something else— unless your occult or personality theory requires it.

What *is* important in our dreams is what they tell us *right now* about what is in our consciousness, in our awareness, about ourselves. What they tell us about ourselves *exactly in the terms of the dream—our terms.* And what is also important is the images they give us, images that we can work with, follow, and enter through visualizations.

One external word of interpretation, one theory-bound probe into the so-called symbols, and the dream ceases to be ours.

We often allow these external probes and interpretations because we believe that "authority" knows more about us than we do. Familiar? The old ghost of dependency again. Let's scrap the idea that *anybody* can see our dreams more clearly than we can. Maybe someone can *theorize* about them better than we can, using a lot of analytic language; but that's just a complication. We are after *simplicity.* Not simple-mindedness. Clean simplicity.

It's a well-known observation that clients in Freudian analysis have sexual dreams; clients in Jungian analysis dream in mythological images; and clients in analysis with exponents of "interpersonal" theories dream forests of people—or no people, in which case these clients are supposed to be in a lot of trouble.

Let's see what we dream all by ourselves, without theories—and let's see what our dreams can tell us about ourselves in *meaningful* ways.

Actually, they might be able to tell us almost everything, and that's why I've saved them for last—for the ultimate journey to the connection of the soul.

"PRIMITIVE" SOCIETIES

Many of the so-called "primitive" cultures of the past— even older cultures which still exist today in some form —dealt with dreams in a direct, meaningful, and rich way. They didn't work with dreams *mainly* in a therapeutic setting; they simply believed that an awareness and understanding of dreams *had* to be therapeutic in the normal course of daily living. Simply that being in touch with the inner and outer realities was a hallmark of balance and health. Dreams became therapeutic issues only when someone was split off from his dreams, which were considered the fundamental stuff of movement and creativity. They understood the meaning of imagination, the necessity for it, its spontaneity and its use as a vehicle to the soul.

I am thinking primarily about the Senoi people of Malaysia and our own Iroquois Indians. They knew more about dreams and where they could lead than anyone since—including Freud, most of whose published analyzed dreams are said to have been his own, and who linked dreams tightly to neurosis and to the sexual quicksands of the Victorian age.

Unlike the therapists and theorists, the Senoi and the Iroquois *linked dreams to life,* to its positive, forward, creative motion. And what happened as a result, particularly among the Senoi, was remarkable.

Senoi never waged war, they had no police force because there was no crime to speak of, there was no violence, no rape, no murder, no juvenile delinquency. It was one hell of a civilization—smart enough even to play on the superstitions of surrounding tribes and thus avoid external attack. Quite simply, the Senoi *pretended* to practice a powerful black magic, and their potential enemies fell for the ruse. And they believed it because the Senoi looked so centered, so strong—*and they looked it because they were.*

You see, the Senoi woke in the morning with a dream on their lips: the children told their dreams to their parents, their parents to *their* parents. It was a "dream culture," without drugs or hallucinations—without any artificiality. They just told their dreams to each other and got in touch with what they meant. Some particularly "hidden" dream might be acted out in the waking world until its meaning was grasped. Often it was as simple as this:

> Son: I dreamed I had a fight with my friend. We hit each other and I cut his lip.
>
> Father: Go to your friend and make it up to him. You hit each other and you cut him. Talk to him and see if you are angry at each other. And if so, why?

And it was done.

Compare this with a standard occurrence in our society:

> Daughter: I dreamed I had a fight with my friend. We hit each other and I cut her lip.
>
> Father: It's only a dream. Don't worry about it.

There is a very direct, very meaningful, correlation between lack of awareness and violence on a personal and collective scale.

EXPLORATION: When you dream of a person you know, tell that person your dream. Ask that person what he or she feels about it. Share *your* feelings and thoughts about it. Do this Exploration with people who are close to you; peripheral acquaintances won't understand or will have difficulties with your explanations. Your family and friends might listen more carefully. Remember that a dream involving a person who in waking life doesn't seem *that* important is telling you quite the contrary. That person is far more important to you than you've thought; so important that he or she has entered deeply inside you. But *you* might not have entered so deeply inside the other person. Nevertheless, you can certainly share your dream with such a person if you wish to.

Whatever you do, see what your discussion leads to in terms of deepening your understanding of your relationship to the dreamed-of person.

Let's avoid the almost reflexive temptation to say that we're too busy or there's not enough time for such discussions. We have to make the time. Not being in touch on this level has brought us to the polar opposite of the Senoi: wholesale violence and misdirected rage.

That the Senoi may have been largely exterminated during World War II shouldn't be a deterrent in following their brilliant lead. Extermination is effected by power-crazed men who have the upper hand technologically. The *spirit* of the Senoi (and of the Iroquois) is as little destroyed as is the spirit of the Jews despite the Nazi holocaust. You can't fight crazy people with planes and guns if you don't have planes and guns.

In America we have more planes and guns than anybody in the world. But maybe we won't have to use them if something better comes along. No one will hurt us at this point in time if we achieve inner understanding and peace.

And no one will hurt us individually.

Now: before you share your dream with a member of your family or with a friend, just see what occurred in it. You might be amazed that you feel anger, or even special affection, for this person. (It isn't terribly uncommon for someone who says he hates his mother to have a dream in which there is obvious affection between them.) Note it. Then get into it with the person. If there are puzzling details, you can both discuss them. Don't play an analytic game of "guessing" what's "behind" it all: stick only to what's there, what the dream *says*.

"Takes courage," you might be thinking.

Yes it does. It takes courage. What exploration of *any* kind doesn't?

Like this one, a fairly common dream, a dream that has many variations. Falling, flying—but especially falling.

EXPLORATION: Whenever you have a "falling" dream, which in our society often ends with an abrupt, even shocking, bolt out of sleep, note it immediately. Jot it down and keep it by the side of your bed. Read it every night before going to sleep and tell yourself that you will have another falling dream and that *you will let yourself fall all the way down*.

You may be asking: "How is it possibe to control my dreaming that way?" You're not controlling anything. You're simply *guiding* yourself. And why not? Who can possibly be a better guide than you?

Let yourself fall in your dream and see what and

whom you meet when you land. Just let it happen. *See what's deep inside.*

THE NOW OF DREAMS

Dreams are very much *Now.* They tell us exactly what's in our deepest consciousness *at any given moment of time.* What's been there yesterday may not be there today—so that if we keep "interpreting" the same dream for any lengthy period, we are involved in past business, and therefore are asking to be stuck in the past.

As far as I'm concerned, too many therapists believe that the dreams they hear on Monday, dreamed by their clients on Friday, are still very much alive. They aren't. They're as dead as yesterday's newspaper: the words are still there but the vitality is gone. Of course similar themes may come back in future dreams, and a dream may be repeated in almost identical form. But any particular dream, once dreamt, is dead the minute it's over—and the *whole* person's consciousness has turned to something else. In my experience, very few people understand this—or look at it in this way. They treat dreams as solid rocks, as monuments to forever—and that misses the essential point that we are always moving. Focusing on yesterday's dreams serves only to keep you stuck—and this is one of the pitfalls of any sort of "talk" therapy.

There's no mystery about it. All we have to do is stop playing games with symbols, stop looking for other meanings; what's there is there. We just have to look. Forget thinking, intellectual exercises, and theories—and *just look.*

My client has a brief dream in which her dominating father is drowning. She cries for help but no one comes. She can't swim and so can't make any effort to save him. The dream ends.

Now, the "game": I've repeated this dream to several colleagues, most of whom immediately interpreted it as a reflection of my client's anger at her father. Note that there is *no anger* in this short dream. One suggested that her father might be a symbol of *me*. Note also that *I* am *not* in the dream. Most thought that her inability to save her father from her own anger created tremendous guilt. Again, there is *no* guilt expressed in this dream. There was also a lot of conjecturing about the meaning of her inability to swim.

What she understood her dream to say, in the context of the *now* of her awareness, is simply this: Her father is drowning or sinking or even about to die in his own territory or medium—which in the dream happens to be water. Unable to swim, she has no place or skills in this medium, she has no business in his drowning world, and she can't help him, she must let him go. And that's all. Yet so much —if one will only look.

It's a good, solid, positive dream. She is letting her father go—and if he's dying or sinking, he's doing it to himself and it has nothing to do with her (if she plunged into the water she would herself drown). She cries out for help. Guilt? It's her *father* who's drowning, a human being. She might indeed have problems if she enjoyed the sight of a drowning man.

EXPLORATION: Look at your next dream. Write it down if this helps to keep it clear. Look at your dream as if it's a real event, a real happening—real in the sense of its taking place in the everyday concrete world. Whatever is there is in your consciousness right now—or at least at the moment you dreamed, *close to* right now, the closest we can ever get to the dream once we wake.

What's the scene? If there are people in the dream, who are they? If there are objects in the dream, what are they?

Now what to do with all this? What's the message? Watch:

• A former client of mine, a professional man, worked extremely long hours and vacationed for four consecutive weeks each summer. Within a month after his vacation he would become oppressively tired; the vacation didn't seem to help at all, and although he enjoyed his work he would begin to clock time until the following summer. Several times during his long year he would dream of beaches, of mountains, of sitting in sidewalk cafés drinking wine. True to the aura of his work "ethic" he regarded these dreams as escapism. Until he realized that he was telling himself, in these dreams, that he required a different vacation schedule. He began to space out his holidays—a week in winter, a week in the spring, two weeks in summer. He was no longer tired throughout the year; and his "escape" dreams, having accomplished their mission, vanished. Simple-minded? Not when you think your tiredness is a product of emotional illness; not when you wonder if you "unconsciously" hate your solid job; and not when you have spent thousands of dollars analyzing your "need" to escape from the "real" world into fantasy.

Dreams will tell you *what* you need. And sometimes even how to get it:

• A friend, also needing a vacation but essentially broke at the time, dreams that he is in an airline terminal being mugged by an ex-wife to whom (in waking life) he pays a huge alimony. She is annoyed that his wallet is empty of money, and annoyed that she can't use his credit cards, all of which are in his name. Disgustedly, she walks away. Shortly after waking, my friend books a two-week trip to Paris. Using his credit cards, he "flies now, pays later." And he begins to negotiate a more adequate alimony settlement.

• Another friend, who loves his car and, as he says, "feels at one with it" when he drives, dreams that his mechanic is very concerned that the car is being run into the ground because it is being driven too hard. And besides, it needs some body work. My friend takes the dream clue, stops denying that he feels sluggish and that his stomach is always sour, sees a doctor for a checkup, makes some effort to slow down his daily pace, and joins a gym for some "body work."

• A married client dreams she is manhandled and raped by a rough, brutal man. She looks at this dream for a long time because it has recurred a number of times. And then there is a kind of "Eureka!" She calmly tells her husband that she has gotten in touch with something about their love-making: she finds him rough, brusque, in a hurry. She doesn't accuse him; she merely asks if he can change. And he tries.

• An interviewer in the personnel section of a large impersonal insurance company dreams that she is lying on a bed in a home for the aged. Her hands are wrinkled and veined, unknown people pass back and forth, and she is despairingly tired. Eventually she leaves her job and takes a new one more suited to her real interests, a more personal setting in which she can feel young and creative.

• A woman has always been disappointed by the men in her life—all highly intellectual, emotionally controlled, "upper-class," polished types. Suave, older men. She has never been their top priority and has always been criticized and put down by them: not educated enough, never read the right books, and all the rest. Finally she has a dream that takes place on a farm. A young man, bare-chested, begins to sow a field. He suddenly turns to her, mops the sweat from his face, and says: "Want to help me plant?" She does so and wakes from the dream exhilarated. She understands that what she has truly needed is a relationship with a young man with whom she can grow.

Are we getting the idea here?

I have no doubt that this short list of dreams might form the core of a book for theoretical flights into symbolism, hidden meanings, etc., etc., and it would be 500 pages of pure academic conjecture. And those pages would not tell us *one thing* about connecting with our souls, about our flesh-blood-spirit lives, or how we can live in a happier, richer, and more fulfilled way.

Our dreams move: they make statements, point out directions, inform us about our depths. And they are exactly what they are. Even dreams that seem weird, bizarre, unfathomable scenes from Dali paintings—even *those* dreams can tell us something about our consciousness at the moment. That is, it might help us a whole lot to *know* that we feel weird, are confused, don't have answers to something, and are seeing aspects of our lives in distorted ways. Because how am I going to straighten out anything if I don't first realize that's it's crooked?

Now if there are gods in your dreams, or goddesses, or strange animals, or mystical places, whatever—just be content that all these forces, all these characters, are within you. You're rich, wealthy. They comprise your power, the sources of your energy, the routes to the soul.

To know that there is a Zeus within you is to connect with the power your Zeus generates.

To pretend, as some analysts might, that your Zeus is a "symbol" of your father turns you into a fool. More, it is a murder of your reality. *Because it has absolutely no basis in what is.*

EXPLORATION: You might want to focus on the familiar people in your dreams. It's always important when people you know pop up during sleep.

Do you have any unfinished business with any of them? Something you might want to say to them? Do you miss someone? Bead in on these possibilities. And then, if you want, convert them into action in your waking life.

An old familiar face might drift by. Someone you haven't seen in years. What happened to the relationship? Want to call the person? If you thought the relationship was over, what about it are you still hanging on to?

Have you killed someone in a dream? What's *that* about? Isn't there some way, some more productive way, you can handle the relationship, your feelings, after waking up?

That's all.

No mysteries.

Just clarity, truth, and the soul-connection between our inner and outer worlds.

DREAM VISUALIZATION

This—the area of dream visualization—is a tricky one because it's enormously powerful and deep, and I have always done it *with* others before I or they have gone on to do it alone. I'm reminded of the age-old warnings that profound meditational practice requires the initial presence and instruction of a guru; that LSD should never be taken while alone; that marijuana is best smoked in the company of friends. Personally, although I believe it about LSD because I've seen some of its effects, I can't *swear* to the truth of any of this—but the warnings are usually rooted in the idea that we might become terribly frightened by the unknown, by people and things that might "leap out" at us. But by this time, if you've done the Explorations, a lot of the unknown is no longer the unknown. By this time you might have developed a taste for it.

So let me introduce you to dream visualization and you can use your own judgment. Take it where you will. If you want to learn of its *uses in psychotherapy,* or its use *as* a therapy, I can direct you to sources of information. But right now, those uses are outside the scope or purpose of this book.

First off, a dream visualization, like the other Explorations, leads you into uncharted waters of great depth. It can be *extremely* spontaneous, yet it's always under your control, the control of your creative consciousness.

EXPLORATION: Start with a simple night dream, one whose imagery appealed to you, a dream you can say you "liked" or that left you with a good feeling.

Now, *very important,* after you close your eyes, relax, and focus for a time on your breathing, place yourself in your setting, your context—the place you've established in your previous visualizations as your "good" place. Then let yourself drift into the scene of the dream—drift, walk, whatever. Through a door, even through a wall.

When you arrive in the dream scene, remember that *anything* is possible, anything can happen, and that you are in full control as the agent of the action. Just let go and do anything you wish.

Let's say there's a beautiful tree in the original night dream, laden with fruit, and you simply looked at it. Now in your dream visualization you have the opportunity to climb the tree, to go up into it. Do it. Become an expert climber (remember that everything is possible in the world of inner reality, and if you can change within, the outer world will also change for you). Or leap up, or fly up—*whatever seems right*. Eat a fruit. Or if there were no fruit in the night dream, go ahead and create them. Taste the fruit. Smell it. *Use all your senses*—the sense of your active imagination being the *major* sense you are using now. *The imagination is our internal "organ" of sense.*

And, of course, if there are people in your night dream, go ahead and hold dialogues with them, find out what you can learn and sense from them. You can see the infinite possibilities here.

Now, lastly: When you have satisfied your curiosity, and have experienced what you have wanted to experience, and wish to return to everyday reality, follow these steps:

1. Keep your eyes closed;
2. Let the images you've seen inwardly drift slowly past your consciousness without pausing or holding on to any of them;
3. Tell yourself that you can re-enter the scene if ever you wish to;
4. Put yourself back into your setting, your inner place;
5. Focus again on your breathing;
6. Feel your body solidly sitting in the chair, feet on the floor, etc.;

7. Become aware of room noises;
8. Then, after a minute or two, slowly open your eyes.

Do these dream visualizations as often as you wish. Sooner or later, depending on your individual pace, the developing possibilities in your inner reality will begin to flow into outer reality. The inner-outer connection, the energy of the soul, will gradually and steadily strengthen.

And remember, as with the visualizations described in the last chapter, it might take some time to stop "watching" yourself and become a fully active, *seeing*, present, participating person—fully involved. It just requires some practice time.

VISUALIZING THE "BAD" DREAM

As I pointed out, there really is no such thing as a "bad" dream *in and of itself*. It's a product of thought and value judgment. Nevertheless, it requires a great deal of courage, risk, and curiosity to go ahead and enter such a dream scene.

By now, you might have the experience that such thoughts are indeed illusions—*but if you have the slightest hesitation, don't plunge into the "bad" dream. Don't hurry or push.* As with everything else, you have to find your pace.

Instead, continue to visualize the comfortable dreams. The more of these you do, the more actively you practice, the less mysterious dreams become in general. Yesterday's "bad" dream may be tomorrow's piece of cake.

As a general governing principle in establishing your soul-connection (and like the growth from infancy to adulthood), remember that you can't skip steps, you can't fly before you walk. You need to establish a footing of comfort and centeredness in one place before moving on to the next.

And if or when you decide to explore an uncomfortable dream, follow all the usual steps involved in entering and leaving the night-dream scenes—all the steps we've outlined. Remember, too, that you can take anyone or anything with you into the visualization. Anything you can use to help you confront the images with the least amount of nervousness. If, for example, you've found a guide in the visualizations, take him, her, or it, with you on the journey. Take a magic potion with you; an amulet; a suit of armor; a mystical sword—whatever you wish. And you can also ask a friend to sit with you in the room while you visualize.

But don't try to fly before you can walk.

I am very serious about this.

Have a great trip!

12
End and
Beginning

It's been a long journey, but let's see it really as only a beginning of the most important voyage we can make. A voyage into ourselves, a never-ending voyage.

A ceaseless process like the sway of the moon over the oceans, the nourishment of the sun on all growing things.

And here you might be interested in a final word from Mark. He writes:

> I continue to develop the Explorations and continue to invent new ones that have meaning for me. I feel that there looms on the horizon, like the golden ball of a beautiful sunrise, one final exploration. Maybe the truly ultimate one. No, I *know* it's the ultimate one. And that is: know exactly how you want to live—and then live that way.

It can be done.
With soul.

Postscript

The Explorations in this book are meant only to expand personal awareness and consciousness, and to make a connection with our inner energy—a connection I call the soul.

They are not meant to alleviate or overcome severe emotional problems or severe emotional pain—in short, they are not meant to substitute for a meaningful psychotherapeutic relationship. The growth of awareness can only be carried out effectively when we are not overwhelmed by intense distress such as a profound depression or ever-present anxiety. In that sense there can be no substitute for a healing relationship with another person. Also, I think it follows just via common sense that a person who is suffering intense emotional pain is not going to be able to focus enough attention or energy to stay with our Explorations.

From another direction: so very many people these days are seeking spiritual development and enlightenment, and are gravitating toward mystic disciplines, particularly those of the East which have found thriving homes in the United States. A small number of these people achieve at least some of their goals. The vast majority don't—and I strongly suspect, a suspicion based on experience and observation, that the failure to achieve these spiritual goals results from an attempt to shortcircuit emotional problems by soaring off into the *ether* of spirituality.

It can't be done. A hungry person must first be fed before he or she can feel the freedom to pursue the contemplation of, say, a beautiful sunrise or a beautiful painting. A crippling phobia can't be dissolved by the pursuit of some cosmic connection.

I hope you get my point.

And one thing more: if you truly feel that you have a major emotional problem that is damaging your life, I have a special Exploration for you:

Act. Get help. It's not a disgrace to have the good sense to help yourself. But it *is* a disgrace, and a great waste, to squander even a moment of our very precious lives.

References

Paul Hawken. *The Magic of Findhorn.* New York: Harper & Row, 1975.

Stephen Larsen. *The Shaman's Doorway.* New York: Harper & Row, 1976.

Peter Tompkins and Christopher Bird. *The Secret Life of Plants.* New York: Harper & Row, 1973.

Lyall Watson. *Gifts of Unknown Things.* New York: Simon & Schuster, 1976.

Arthur M. Young. *The Reflexive Universe.* New York: Delacorte Press, 1976.